Fires of Consciousness:
The Tao of Onliness I Ching

by
Martin Treon

i

From *Sex, Ecology, Spirituality: The Spirit of Evolution* by Ken Wilber, © 1995. Reprinted by arrangement with Shambhala Publications, Inc., 300 Massachusetts Avenue, Boston, MA. 02115.

From *Eye to Eye: The Quest for a New Paradigm* by Ken Wilber, © 1983, 1990, 1996. Reprinted by arrangement with Shambhala Publications, Inc., 300 Massachusetts Avenue, Boston, MA. 02115.

Auroral Skies Press
Vermillion, South Dakota

1996

Copyright 1996 by Martin Treon
All rights reserved. Printed in the United States of America

Book Manufacture /Production by:
BookCrafters
140 Buchanan
P.O. Box 370
Chelsea, MI 48118

By Mail: Order from:
BookCrafters Order Department
P.O. Box 459
Chelsea, MI 48118

By Phone: (Ordering Only): 1-800-879-4214
The price is $14.95 (add $4.00
shipping and handling/single copy and
$1.00 each additional copy)

Photography by Martin Treon
Typography by Elizabeth Simmons
Cover Design by Martin Treon and Elizabeth Simmons

LIBRARY OF CONGRESS CATALOGING-IN PUBLICATION DATA

Treon, Martin, 1937-
   Fires of Consciousness: The Tao of Onliness I Ching / Martin Treon

ISBN # 0-9655740-4-0 $14.95

1 Consciousness   2 I Ching   3 Zen Buddhism

Library of Congress Catalog Card Number: 96-95029

PUBLISHED BY AURORAL SKIES PRESS, 18 FOREST AVE., VERMILLION, SOUTH DAKOTA 57069

Table of Contents

"And the angel of the LORD appeared unto him in a flame of fire out of the midst of a bush: and he looked, and, behold, the bush burned with fire, and the bush *was* not consumed.

And Moses said, I will now turn aside, and see this great sight, why the bush is not burnt.

And when the LORD saw that he turned aside to see, God called unto him out of the midst of the bush, and said, Moses, Moses. And he said, Here *am* I.

And he said, Draw not nigh hither: put off thy shoes from thy feet, for the place whereon thou standest *is* holy ground. . .

And Moses said unto God, Behold, *when* I come unto the children of Israel, and shall say unto them, The God of your fathers hath sent me unto you, and they shall say to me, What *is* his name? what shall I say unto them?

And God said unto Moses, I AM THAT I AM: and he said, Thus shalt thou say unto the children of Israel, I AM hath sent me unto you."

- The Holy Bible (King James Version)
Exodus, Chapter Three,
Verses 2, 3, 4, 5, 13, and 14

"If you push forward with your last ounce of strength at the very point where the path of your thinking has been blocked, and then, completely stymied, leap with hands high in the air into the tremendous abyss of fire confronting you - into the ever-burning flame of your own primordial nature - all ego-consciousness, all delusive feelings and thoughts and perceptions will perish with your ego-root and the true source of your Self-nature will appear."

- Bassui's letter to Layman Ippo
from *The Three Pillars of Zen*
by Roshi Philip Kapleau (Editor)

CHAPTER ONE

The Seed-Core of Tao of Onliness:

Trans-istent, Omnistent, Arch-istent, and Prim-istent Realities

I

"*Searching for the Ox*. The beast has never gone astray, and what is the use of searching for him? The reason why the oxherd is not on intimate terms with him is because the oxherd himself has violated his own inmost nature. The beast is lost, for the oxherd has himself been led out of the way through his deluding senses. His home is receding farther away from him, and byways and crossways are ever confused. Desire for gain and fear of loss burn like fire; ideas of right and wrong shoot up like a phalanx.
    Alone in the wilderness, lost in the jungle, the boy is
        searching, searching!
    The swelling waters, the far-away mountains, and the
        unending path;
    Exhausted and in despair, he knows not where to go,
    He only hears the evening cicadas singing in the
        maple-woods."

-from "The Ten Oxherding Pictures"
by Kaku-an
-compiled by D. T. Suzuki
from *Manual of Zen Buddhism*

"At the psychic level, the universalizing and global tendencies of reason and vision-logic come to fruition in a direct experience—initial, preliminary, but unmistakable—of a truly universal Self, common in and to all beings; . . . so much so that this Self is understood to be prior to, within, and beyond matter, life, and mind. . . . —the Over-Soul as the World Soul in the commonwealth of all beings as an objective State of Affairs."

-Ken Wilber
from *Sex, Ecology, Spirituality: The Spirit of Evolution*
(see Appendix C)

In surf-spray among the seagulls
on the beach close to the water
learned man and recluse woman walk.
With the tide of daylight ebbing,
late afternoon turning to evening,
as they amble now along the shore.

Solitary silent figures,
side by side strolling together.
Resounding surf in rhythmic pattern
driven by enormous breakers
pound the shore and make it shudder.

Above the beach are rolling sand dunes
sparsely clad in shrubs and grasses.
To the shelter of one sand dune
walk the recluse and the drifter.
Here they sit beside each other
where the breaking surf is quiet
and the vista of the sea is far.

Here the twilight fades to darkness

as they look out on the ocean

with its giant moon ascending.

For a long while they sit silent

viewing this great sea of moonlight

and the ocean breaking on the shore.

Recluse: Learned vagabond, you stumble on in darkness

of mental attribution shadows.

Asleep in thought illusion,

stranded in vacant worlds.

Beloved, what emptiness your Heart must long endure.

A long silence rests between them.

The salt-scent of seabreeze fills the air.

Learned one (Lo): Sage, what you say about me is so true.

But this is what I understand and know,

these intimations I call Onliness.

They *are* thoughts of egoic consciousness;

conceiver and conceived duality.

This is a time of profound change for me.

A time of dying and of being Born.

A turning and returning so complete

that I come face to face with my own death

and Know it as the phantom that it is.

Know Consciousness undying and unborn;

That which I ever Am, have Been, shall Be.

My vacant ego life is endless night

with only glimpses of another Way.

I view the folly of my life unfold

churned up and stirring from some venal depth.

Night after night my dreams cry out to me,

clear and powerful, grim and raging dreams.

In these shattered mirrors I view myself,

see self-indulgent vanity and fear.

Yet in it all a cleansing seems to be,

a modest ebbing of egoic tide.

Learned one turns and looks at recluse

who is gazing out upon the sea.

He then lies back upon the sand.

Lo: I have devised an I Ching supplement

with distinct text, image, and expression

for each of its sixty-four hexagrams.

This is the Tao of Onliness I Ching.

This Consciousness Itself Cosmology.

Primarily, Onliness emerges

from Taoist and Zen Buddhist Perspective.

Indeed, Onliness is a Way of Zen.

Of the Perennial Philosophy,

It also derives from and returns to

the mystic transcendental insight Streams

of Christianity, Hinduism,

Judaism, Islam, the Baha'i Faith,

and Native American Streams as well.

Onliness Itself is Unknowable.

Within Pan-gnostic Existential Realm,

Knowledge and Compassion mark Onliness.

Egoic self-importance dies away.

Onliness Tao is plain and bland indeed.

Its Path is of the Way of everyday.

Its Heart is very old and very new.

Its Namelessness is of the Watercourse.

It's deeply rooted in eternal Tao.

Yet as cosmology It goes by name,

this is concession to duality.

But that *named* emerges from the Nameless

and thus so named, returns to Namelessness.

In metaphor, through Existential eyes,

nothing named is literal or complete.

This Onliness Insight and Mindfulness

is Fact Itself, intuitively Known.

There is no question of this Knowingness,

It is transcendent and not relative.

Drifter sits up and looks about.

Recluse looks out on the moonlit sea.

Lo: As a conceptual cosmology,

it is no more than dust upon the wind.

Sage, only a dead skin that must be shed.

Tao of Onliness is a Vehicle;

not at all an answer but a Question.

Expressed through egoic duality,

Its Essence is yet Nonduality.

As expressed, clinging discrimination,

yet Its Heart is Nondiscrimination.

In expression, a conceptual "thing",

Its Message is No-thingness and No-mind.

Expressed as if It were attainable,

Its Path is non-attainment, non-striving.

Nothing to see, no one there to see it.

This Illuminative Cosmology.

Rooted in Non-action, Non-attachment.

Onliness Tao, the Truth It has to say

and Consciousness, the Body of that Truth.

Transcendental, *all* Realms of Onliness;

each One transcends space-time reality.

Revelation, the Way of Its accord.

Intuition and Righteousness, Its Eyes

and Onliness, Its viewed Reality.

This *Self* of All-embracing Onliness.

Tao of Onliness Zen Enlightenment:

This birthless, deathless Self of Consciousness.

This boundless Buddhahood of Self-nature.

Drifter takes two papers from his pack

and puts these on the ground before them.

Lo: In Tao of Onliness cosmology

eternal, nameless Tao is Ultimate. (Treon, 1989)

Tao can't be pictured in these diagrams

(pointing to Figures 1 and 2 on the ground).

Arising from, returning to the Tao

is *Consciousness*, This Tao Inherency;

Tao Incarnate, but *not* eternal Tao.

This *Self* of Unconditionality.

Buddha-nature, Brahman, Christ-consciousness.

The *whole* surface of these two diagrams

as well as their ink and paper substance

(gesturing to these papers on the ground)

symbolize ineffable Consciousness.

All pervasive-inclusive Consciousness.

This unmediated Enlightenment.

This unbounded and uncreated Self.

Consciousness Itself is Trans-manifest:

thus Manifest and/or Unmanifest,

not Manifest and/or Unmanifest,

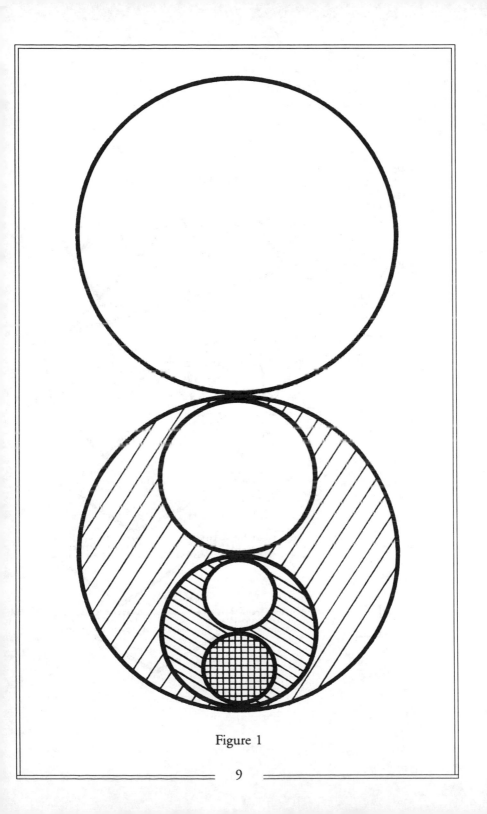

Figure 1

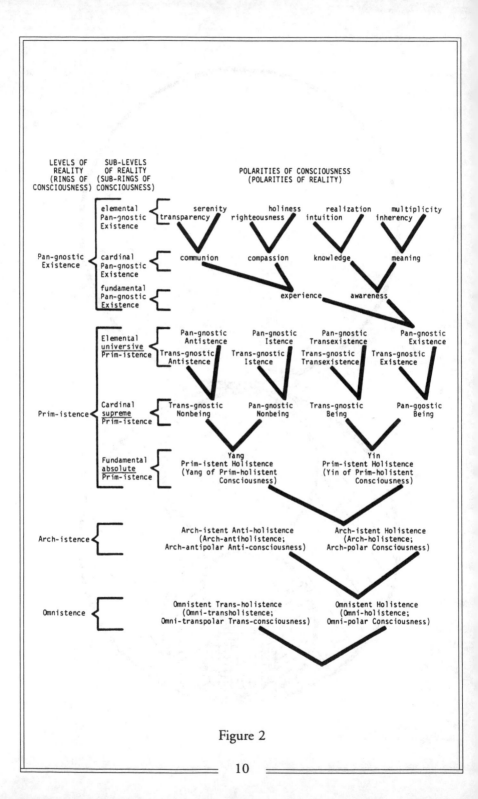

Figure 2

not, not. . ., not, not not. . ., and not, not not not. . .

Trans-istence Itself, without a second.

Trans-istent Absolute Reality.

Unspeakable No-thingness and No-mind.

Unfathomable Truth of Onliness.

Sage, Consciousness Only, Only, Only. . .

Wind from the sea gusts through the dunes.

Learned one gets up and walks about,

through the dunes and down along the beach.

Breakers cast a phosphorescent glow.

Foothills bathed in moonlight can be seen

rising from the sand dunes of the shore.

Drifter returns and sits by recluse.

Recluse scoops up sand into her hand

and watches it slip through her fingers.

Lo: *Omnistent* Consciousness Reality

   (pointing to the two largest circles of Figure 1, then to this Realm in Figure 2)

   arises from, returns to Consciousness.

   This *Unmanifest* Omnistential Realm

   as Seen through Manifest Existence eyes.

   Unmanifest Omnist Polarity

   between *Omnistent polar Consciousness*

   (pointing to the lower largest circle of Figure 1, then to this Realm in Figure 2)

   and *Omnist transpolar Trans-consciousness*

(pointing to the upper largest circle of Figure 1, then to this Realm in Figure 2).

Omni-conscious, Omni-transconsciousness.

Omnistent Absolute Polarity.

This *most* profound Polarity of all.

Primal Polarity of Consciousness:

between Omnistent Holistential Realm,

this Omni-holistent Reality

(pointing to the lower largest circle of Figure 1, then to this Realm in Figure 2),

and Omnistent Trans-holistential Realm,

Omni-transholistent Reality

(pointing to the upper largest circle of Figure 1, then to this Realm in Figure 2).

Holistence is *holonic* polar Self. (Wilber, 1995)

What is Omnistent polar Consciousness?

It's Absolute Polarity's Yin *Form*

as Seen through Pan-gnostic Existence eyes

(pointing to the lower largest darkened circle of Figure 1).

Ineffable Polar Reality,

illuminating Eye of the I Ching.

As Seen through Pan-gnostic Existence eyes,

Omnistent transpolar Trans-consciousness

is Absolute Polarity's Yang *Void*

(pointing to the upper largest white circle in Figure 1).

This unfathomable Transpolar Realm.

Beyond beyondness, what more can I say?

A cool seabreeze blows through the dunes.

Recluse lies back upon the sand

and looks at the tropic stars above.

Head lowered, drifter seems lost in thought.

They repose in silence for a time.

Rising up, recluse walks away.

She gathers driftwood along the shore.

Returning, she stacks it on the sand.

Drifter gets up and gathers brush.

Piling dry driftwood on this brush,

he strikes a match and ignites a flame.

Both sit down before the bright fire.

Lo: Arising from and thence returning to

> Omnistent Holistent Reality

> (pointing to the lower largest circle of Figure 1, then to this Realm in Figure 2)

> is this *Arch-istential* Consciousness Realm

> (pointing to the two second largest circles of Figure 1, then to this

> Realm in Figure 2).

> This Unmanifest Arch-istential Realm

> Seen through Manifest Existential eyes.

> Omni-holistence's Polarity

> (pointing to this relationship in Figure 2).

> Unmanifest Arch-ist Polarity

> between *Arch-istent Holistential* Realm,

> which is *Arch-istent polar Consciousness*

> (pointing to the lower second largest circle of Figure 1, then to this

Realm in Figure 2),

and *Arch-istent Anti-holistent* Realm,

this *anti-polar Anti-consciousness*

(pointing to the upper second largest circle of Figure 1, then to this

Realm in Figure 2).

Arch-holistence, Arch-antiholistence.

Arch-consciousness, Arch-anticonsciousness.

Arch-istent Transparent Polarity.

Final Unmanifest Polarity.

This *last* transcendental Polarity

completely beyond Manifestation.

What is Arch-istent polar Consciousness?

It's Transparent Polarity's Yin *Form*

as Seen through Pan-gnostic Existence eyes

(pointing to the lower second largest darkened circle of Figure 1).

Ineffable polar Arch-holistence.

Wellspring of Prim-istent Reality.

What is Arch-istent Anti-holistence?

As seen through Pan-gnostic Existence eyes,

It's Transparent Polarity's Yang *Void*

(pointing to the upper second largest white circle of Figure 1).

Beyond Arch-conscious *polar* Conception.

Recluse woman looks into the flame.

Drifter gazes out upon the sea.

Moonlit seagulls cry out overhead
and distant waves break along the shore.

Learned one adds wood to the fire.
Sparks from the flame rise into the night.
He looks on as the fire grows.

Recluse takes a sack from the backpack.
Out of it come salmon sandwiches,
peanuts, pineapple chunks, sliced carrots,
and a jar filled with pineapple juice.
Silently they share this night repast.

After clean-up drifter stands and yawns.
Extending his arms, he looks at the moon
Recluse stretches out upon the sand.

Drifter walks about among the dunes,
watching gulls and listening to surf.
Recluse is asleep when he returns.
Drifter appears not to notice this.
He sits down before the dancing flame.
Lo: Sage, arising from and returning to
        Arch-holistential polar Consciousness
        (pointing to the lower second largest circle of Figure 1, then to this
        Realm in Figure 2)
        is this Realm of *Prim-istent Holistence*

(pointing to the two smallest circles of Figure 1, then to these Yin-Yang Realms in Figure 2).

Prim-istent *absolute* Reality

(pointing to this sub-Realm in Figure 2).

Polarity of Holistence Itself;

Holonic polar Self Polarity.

Polarity of polar Consciousness.

All Prim-istence is polar Consciousness

Seen through Pan-gnostic Existential eyes

(pointing to Prim-istence in Figure 2).

Although Prim-istence Ground, Its Deep Structure,

which is Unfathomable Namelessness,

is of *Unmanifest* Reality,

Its Face, or Surface Structure, here described

(gesturing to the Levels and Polarities of Prim-istence pictured in Figure 2)

is at least *potentially Manifest.*

This *absolute* Prim-ist Polarity

(pointing to this Yin-Yang Polarity in Figure 2)

between *Yin Prim-istent Holistence* Realm -

this *Origin* and *Source* of Being's Realm

(pointing to the lower smallest darkened circle of Figure 1, then to this Realm in Figure 2).

and *Yang Prim-istent Holistential* Realm -

this *Origin* and *Source* of Nonbeing

(pointing to the upper smallest white circle of Figure 1, then to this
Realm in Figure 2).

Yin Prim-holistence, Yang Prim-holistence.

Prim-istent absolute Polarity.

Yin-Yang *absolute* holon-polar Selves.

This deepest, *most* profound Polarity
of Manifest Holistent Consciousness
(pointing to the two smallest circles of Figure 1)
from which bloom sixteen Holistential Realms
of Yin and Yang *absolute* Prim-istence:
Prim-istent *absolute* Realities.

These eight Yin, eight Yang Prim-holistent Realms
flower from *absolute* Polarity
(pointing to the lower smallest Yin circle, then to the upper smallest
Yang circle of Figure 1):
Prim-istent *absolute* Yin and Yang *Am,*
Actlessness, Radiance, Emptiness, Mind,
Awakening, Mystery, Onliness.
Prim-istent *absolute* Polarities.

These Paths of *absolute* Enlightenment,
which *fully* Manifest Enlightenment
are ultimately Merged in Consciousness -
beyond Distinction or Identity.

Recluse woman sleeps upon the sand.

Tropic moon ascends over the sea.

Learned one leans back upon the dune,

staring at the fire's dying flame.

Recluse awakens and sits up.

The fire flares in a gust of wind.

Recluse: Only Self-revelation reveals Reality.

In silence they sit before the flame.

Drifter looks out on vast moonlit sea.

Recluse lifts his papers from the ground

and places these upon the fire.

Drifter turns and looks at the recluse.

Expressionless, recluse turns to him.

From the fire's edge she grabs a stick.

Rising up, she pulls up the drifter.

In her left hand is the burning stick

and at her right arm, the learned one.

She leads him to the breaking surf

and throws the stick into the sea.

The whole ocean instantly ignites!

Everything at once engulfed in flame.

Sea, shore, man, woman, dunes, island, sky -

all of this reality consumed.

The flame alone is and remains.

Slowly it too fades and is no more.

Neither Apparency Appears

nor does Transparency Transpear.

There occurs transcendence *utterly*

of Existence and Transexistence.

Alone, Istential Parency Pears.

Identity Pearing unto Self.

Thusly, only Pearingness "remains".

CHAPTER TWO

The Blooming of Tao of Onliness:
Prim-istent and Pan-gnostic Existent Realities

II

"*Seeing the Traces.* By the aid of the sutras and by inquiring into the doctrines, he has come to understand something, he has found the traces. He now knows that vessels, however varied, are all of gold, and that the objective world is a reflection of the Self. Yet, he is unable to distinguish what is good from what is not, his mind is still confused as to truth and falsehood. As he has not yet entered the gate, he is provisionally said to have noticed the traces.

> By the stream and under the trees, scattered are the
> traces of the lost;
> The sweet-scented grasses are growing thick—did he
> find the way?
> However remote over the hills and far away the beast
> may wander,
> His nose reaches the heavens and none can conceal
> it."

-from "The Ten Oxherding Pictures"
by Kaku-an
-compiled by D. T. Suzuki
from *Manual of Zen Buddhism*

"Suddenly, self-knowing dies (the mute point to the still water next to the
  boat from which a loon, emerging from its watery dive, unexpectedly
  splashes forth), and Revelation unto Self is Born."

Drifter wakens from his reverie.
He had been idly viewing
his reflection in the water
when the loon splashed through the surface,
shattering his image on the lake,
spraying water on his face and shirt.

At once, the large loon dives again.
Drifter nods and smiles to the mute.
The mute man baits his hook with a worm.
White lake gulls cry out overhead,
diving to catch fish from time to time.
A breeze stirs the summer afternoon.
Sunlight glistens on the blue water.
Billowing white clouds float high above.

Mute and learned one fish from a boat

floating in a secluded bay.

Drifter threads a worm upon his hook.

Extending his pole from the boat,

he drops his line into the lake.

Lo: Sage, my life is a carnival of dreams;

kaleidoscopic phantom images

projected on an undulating sea.

Duality of seer and that seen.

Prudently, I cling to and hide within

these images of world-field self.

Afraid of turning from my old routines

and flowering full-bloom without reserve.

Living in the world's house of mirrors,

unconsciously I stumble through this maze

seeking release from it where none exists.

So vast and dark is this egoic night;

so deeply rooted, this egoic dream.

Mute pulls up a full-sized small-mouth bass.

Wide-eyed, drifter gazes at the fish.

Suddenly he feels his line tug

and proceeds to pull in a bluegill.

They put these fish in a wire cage

hanging in the water from the boat.

Baiting their hooks, they resume fishing.

In silence they fish from the boat,

pulling in pan fish from time to time.

A sudden breeze gusts across the boat.

The scent of fish and fresh-water lake

fill the nostrils of the learned one.

Mute looks out across the blue water

glittering in sunlit afternoon.

Drifter finally draws in his line

and puts his fishing gear away.

He takes three papers from his pocket

and puts these before him on the seat.

Mute stops fishing to light up his pipe.

He views drifter, who seems deep in thought.

Lo: These are Realms, sub-Realms, and Polarities

of Consciousness in Tao of Onliness

(gesturing to the whole Figure 2A diagram).

This blooming bush of Tao of Onliness

(gesturing to the flowering bush diagram of Figure 3).

In Tao of Onliness cosmology

(pointing to the bush's base and trunk in Figure 3),

eternal, nameless Tao is Ultimate.

Tao can't be pictured in these diagrams

(gesturing to the three papers before him on the seat).

From Tao, Consciousness arises, returns.

The whole surface of these three diagrams

as well as their paper and ink substance

symbolize this Absolute Consciousness.

Trans-istent Trans-manifest Consciousness.

This All and None and Every and No-thing.

Boundless, birthless, deathless - unspeakable!

Omnistent Consciousness Reality,

this Unmanifest Omnistential Realm

(pointing to this Realm in Figure 2A, then to the two Omnistential

branches of Figure 3),

arises from, returns to Consciousness.

Omnistent Absolute Polarity

of Omni-transpolar Tranconsciousness

and Omnistential polar Consciousness

(pointing respectively to these two polar Realms in Figures 2A and 3).

Arch-istent Consciousness Reality,

this Unmanifest Arch-istential Realm

(pointing to this Realm in Figure 2A, then to the two Arch-istential

branches of Figure 3),

arises from and thence returns back to

Omni-holistent polar Consciousness

(pointing to this relationship in both Figures 2A and 3).

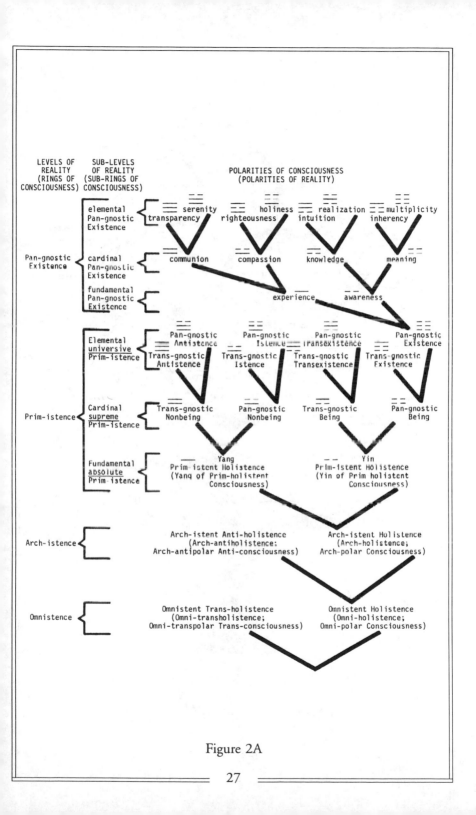

Figure 2A

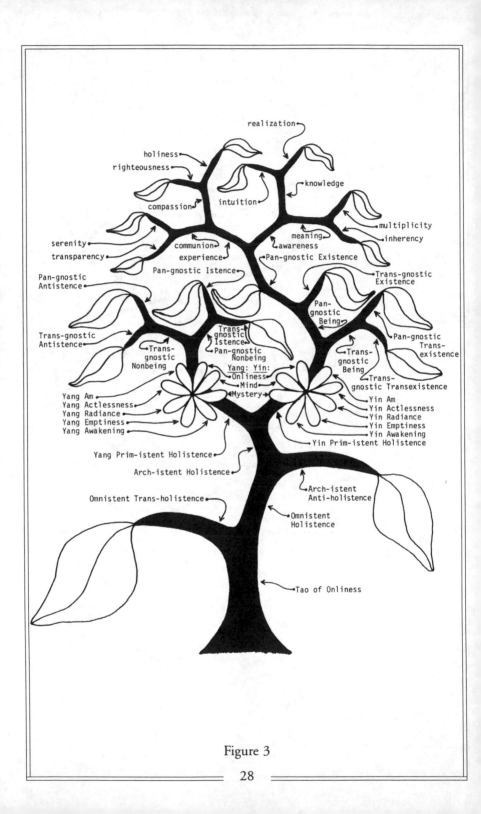

Figure 3

28

Arch-istent Transparent Polarity:

Arch-antipolar Anti-consciousness

and Arch-istential polar Consciousness

(pointing to these two polar Realities in Figures 2A and 3).

Mute's line tightens and his pole bends.

He pulls in and unhooks a large perch,

then puts it into the wire cage.

Drifter looks on admiringly

but soon returns to his diagrams.

Lo: Recall this Yin-Yang holomorphic view (Treon, 1989)

(gesturing to Figure 4).

Six-ringed Pan-gnostic Existence centered

Prim-istent Reality diagram.

This first *absolute* Prim-holistent ring

(his finger circles the sixteen quadrigrams of the fourth ring of Figure 4):

Fundamental *absolute* Prim-istence

(pointing to this sub-Realm in Figure 2A).

This *absolute* Prim-istent Consciousness,

whose Prim-holist Face can be Manifest,

arises from and thence returns back to

Arch-holistential polar Consciousness -

holonic Arch-istential polar Self

(pointing to this relationship in both Figures 2A and 3).

Prim-istent *absolute* Polarity

between Yin Prim-istent *absolute* Realm,

Yin Way of *absolute* Enlightenment,

which Realm is the Spring from which Being flows

(pointing to this Realm in Figure 2A, then to this Yin branch of Figure 3),

and this Yang Prim-istent *absolute* Realm,

Yang Way of *absolute* Enlightenment,

which is the Spring from which Nonbeing flows

(pointing to this Realm in Figure 2A, then to this Yang branch of Figure 3).

Within this *absolute* Polarity

there bloom *sixteen* Prim-ist *absolute* Realms

of *eight* Prim-holistent Polarities,

eight Prim-ist *absolute* Polarities

(pointing alternately to each of the eight Yin and eight Yang flowering

petals of Figure 3, then to the eight directly opposite Yin-Yang

Polarities of the fourth ring of Figure 4).

These absolute polar Consciousness Realms

(starting at the top of the fourth ring of Figure 4 and pointing

counterclockwise around this ring to each of the sixteen quadrigrams

which symbolize each Realm):

Yang Am, Yin Actlessness, Yang Radiance,

Yin Emptiness and Yang Awakening,

Yin Mystery, Yang Mind, Yin Onliness,

Yin Am, Yang Actlessness, Yin Radiance,

Yang Emptiness and Yin Awakening,

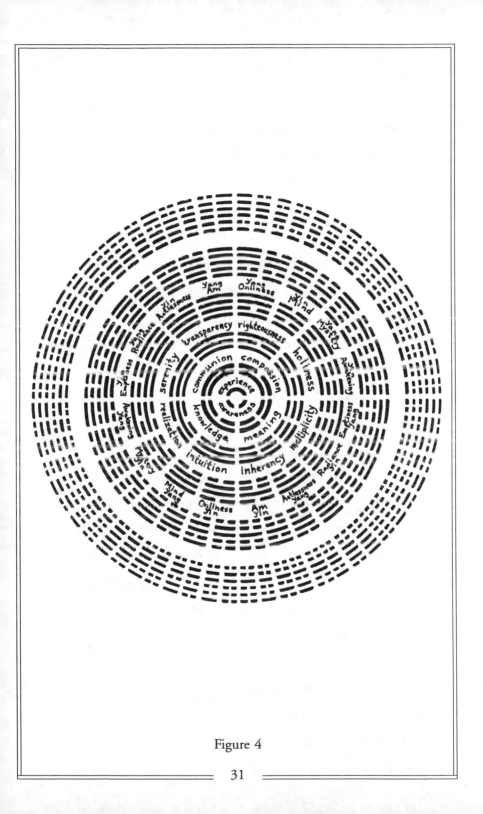

Figure 4

Yang Mystery, Yin Mind, Yang Onliness.

Sixteen Prim-istent Holistential Realms:
Consciousness most profoundly Manifest,
absolute Manifest Reality.
This *Self* of Realized Enlightenment.

These Paths become *One* in Enlightenment,
Merging *completely* in this Consciousness.
Trans-manifest Enlightenment only.
Enlightenment is Consciousness Itself.

Eight Polarities of Enlightenment,
sixteen Enlightenment Realities,
from perspective of Tao of Onliness
as Seen through Pan-gnostic Existent eyes.
These eight Yin-Yang Prim-istential Flowers
(pointing alternately to the sixteen directly opposite Yin-Yang absolute
Realities which comprise the eight absolute Polarities of the fourth
ring of Figure 4, while at the same time including in this gesture the
Yin-Yang patterns of the fifth and sixth rings which derive from each of
these sixteen fourth-ring Realms).
Learned one looks at the ragged mute.
Mute's eyes are closed and he smokes his pipe.
Drifter looks toward the distant shore
lined with tall pines, birch, and maple trees.
A passing cloud shades the two men.

Gulls cry out and waves lap on the boat.

Lo: This second *supreme* Prim-istential ring

(his finger circles the thirty-two pentagrams of the fifth ring of Figure 4)

called Cardinal *supreme* Prim-istent Realm

(pointing to this sub-Realm of Figure 2A).

This *supreme* Prim-istential Consciousness,

whose Face is *potentially* Manifest,

arises from and thence returns back to

Yin and Yang *absolute* Prim-holistence

(pointing to this relationship in Figure 2).

Arising from and thence returning to

Yin Realm of Prim-holistent Consciousness

(pointing to this Reality in Figure 2A, to this branch of Figure 3, then

to the eight fourth-line Yin (– –) symbol quadrigrams of the fourth

ring of Figure 4)

is this Prim-ist *supreme* Polarity

of *Trans-gnostic Being* Reality (==)

(pointing to this Realm in Figure 2A, to this branch of Figure 3, then

to the eight fourth-and-fifth-line Yin-Yang symbol (==) pentagrams

of the fifth ring of Figure 4)

and *Pan-gnostic Being* Reality (= =)

(pointing in this same way to Figures 2A, 3, and 4 respectively).

This Trans- and Pan- gnostic Polarity (== = =)

which is *within* Being Reality

(pointing to this Polarity within Being in Figure 2A, to these two

branches of Figure 3, then to the eight pairs of adjacent pentagrams of the fifth ring of Figure 4 which have this (== = =) fourth-and fifth line Yin-Yang configuration contrast).

Sage, transcendental Realization

across and *as* all Knowingness Itself

from Being *or* Nonbeing Perspective

is what Pan-gnostic means in this context.

Transcendental Trans-realization

as and *beyond* all Knowingness Itself

from Being *or* Nonbeing Perspective

is what Trans-gnostic means in this context.

Arising from and thence returning to

Yang Realm of Prim-holistent Consciousness

(pointing to this Reality in Figure 2A, to this branch of Figure 3, then to the eight fourth-line Yang (—) symbol quadrigrams of the fourth ring of Figure 4)

is this Prim-ist *supreme* Polarity

between this *Trans-gnostic Nonbeing* Realm (==)

(pointing to this Reality in Figure 2A, to this branch of Figure 3, then to the eight fourth-and-fifth-line Yin-Yang symbol (==) pentagrams of the fifth ring of Figure 4)

and this Realm of *Pan-gnostic Nonbeing* (==)

(pointing in this same way to Figures 2A, 3, and 4 respectively).

This Trans- and Pan- gnostic Polarity (== ==)

which inheres *within* this Nonbeing Realm

(pointing to this Polarity within Nonbeing in Figure 2A, to these two

branches of Figure 3, then to the eight pairs of adjacent pentagrams of

the fifth ring of Figure 4 which have this (══ ══) fourth-and

fifth-line Yin-Yang configuration contrast).

Two *supreme* Prim-istent Polarities

exist *between* Being and Nonbeing.

Thus, this *greater supreme* Polarity

between *Pan-gnostic Being* Consciousness (= =)

(pointing to this Reality in Figure 2A, to this branch of Figure 3, then

to the eight fourth-and-fifth-line Yin-Yang greater Hsiang symbol

(= =) pentagrams of the fifth ring of Figure 4)

and *Trans-gnostic Nonbeing* Consciousness (══)

(pointing to this Reality in Figure 2A, to this branch of Figure 3,

then to the eight fourth-and-fifth-line Yin-Yang greater Hsiang

symbol (══) pentagrams which, on the fifth ring of Figure 4, are

directly opposite of the above (═ ═) eight pentagrams).

And this *lesser supreme* Polarity

between Trans-gnostic Being Consciousness (══)

(pointing to this Realm in Figure 2A, to this branch of Figure 3, then

to these eight fourth-and-fifth-line Yin-Yang lesser Hsiang symbol

(══) pentagrams of the fifth ring of Figure 4)

and *Pan-gnostic Nonbeing* Consciousness (══)

(pointing to this Reality in Figure 2, to this branch of Figure 3, then to these eight fourth-and-fifth-line Yin-Yang lesser Hsiang ($\equiv\!\equiv$)

pentagrams which, on the fifth ring of Figure 4, are directly opposite

of the above ($\equiv\!\equiv$) eight pentagrams).

Four *supreme* Prim-istent Polarities:

One *within* Being, One in Nonbeing,

and two *between* Being and Nonbeing

(pointing to these Polarities in Figure 2A).

Mute baits his hook and resumes fishing.

No sooner is his line in the lake

than a fish bites and his pole bends.

The hooked fish struggles to swim away

as mute brings it closer to the boat,

and then scoops it out of the water.

It is a very large bluegill,

biggest the drifter has ever seen.

Mute unhooks it, puts it in the cage.

He then baits and resumes fishing.

Lo: Thus arising from and returning to

these sixteen *absolute* Prim-istent Realms

(pointing to these fourth ring Realms of Figure 4)

are thirty-two *supreme* Prim-istent Realms

(his finger circles the thirty-two pentagrams of the fifth ring of Figure 4)

of transcendent Being and Nonbeing.

From *Yin absolute* Prim-holistent Realms

(pointing to the eight Yin quadrigrams of the fourth ring of Figure 4) spring these *supreme* Prim-istent *Being* Realms

(pointing to the sixteen adjacent pentagrams of the fifth ring with this

fourth-and-fifth-line Yin-Yang configuration (= =   ==) just above

each Yin quadrigram of the fourth ring of Figure 4).

From *Yang absolute* Prim-holistent Realms

(pointing to the eight Yang quadrigrams of the fourth ring of Figure 4),

these *supreme* Prim-istent *Nonbeing* Realms

(pointing to the sixteen adjacent pentagrams of the fifth ring with this

fourth-and-fifth-line Yin-Yang configuration (==   ==) just above

each Yang quadrigram of the fourth ring of Figure 4).

Mute hooks and pulls in a small sunfish.

It flops and splashes about the boat

before mute can get firm hold of it.

Water gets sprayed on drifter's papers.

He quickly sweeps this water off,

then dabs these with his handkerchief.

Mute chuckles and is most amused.

Drifter looks up at him and smiles.

Mute unhooks and throws the fish back in,

then baits his hook and resumes fishing.

Drifter bends over his papers.

Lo: This third *universive* Prim-istent ring

(his finger circles the sixty-four hexagrams of the sixth ring of Figure 4)

called Elemental *universive* Realm

(pointing to this sub-Realm of Figure 2A).

Prim-istent *universal* Consciousness,

whose Surface Structure can be Manifest,

arises from and thence returns back to

Trans-gnostic and Pan-gnostic Nonbeing,

and Trans-gnostic and Pan-gnostic Being

(pointing to this relationship in Figure 2A).

At once emerging from, returning to

this *supreme* Trans-gnostic Nonbeing Realm (⚏)

(pointing to this Reality in Figure 2A, to this branch of Figure 3, then

to the eight fourth-and-fifth-line Yin-Yang symbol (⚏) pentagrams

of the fifth ring of Figure 4):

Prim-ist *universive* Polarity

of *Trans-gnostic Antistence* Consciousness (☷)

 (pointing to this Realm in Figure 2A, to this branch of Figure 3, then

to these eight fourth-fifth-and-sixth-line Yin-Yang symbol (☷)

hexagrams of the sixth ring of Figure 4)

and *Pan-gnostic Antistence* Consciousness (☶)

(pointing to this Reality in Figure 2A, to this branch of Figure 3, then

to these eight fourth-fifth-and-sixth-line Yin-Yang symbol (☶)

hexagrams of the sixth ring of Figure 4).

This Trans- and Pan- gnostic Polarity (☷ ☶)

within Antistential Reality

(pointing to this Polarity within Antistence in Figure 2A, to these two

branches of Figure 3, then to the eight pairs if adjacent hexagrams of

the sixth ring of Figure 4 with this (☷ ☶) fourth-fifth-and

sixth-line Yin-Yang configuration).

Arising from and thence returning to

this *supreme* Pan-gnostic Nonbeing Realm (⚏)

(pointing to this Reality in Figure 2A, to this branch of Figure 3, then

to the eight fourth-and-fifth-line Yin-Yang symbol (⚏) pentagrams

of the fifth ring of Figure 4):

Prim-ist *universive* Polarity

of *Trans-gnostic Istential* Consciousness (⚌)

(pointing to this Realm in Figure 2A, to this branch of Figure 3, then

to the eight fourth-fifth-and-sixth line Yin-Yang symbol (⚌)

hexagrams of the sixth ring of Figure 4)

and *Pan-gnostic Istential* Consciousness (⚎)

(pointing to this Realm in Figure 2A, to this branch of Figure 3, then

to the eight fourth fifth and sixth line Yin-Yang symbol (⚍)

hexagrams of the sixth ring of Figure 4).

This Trans- and Pan- gnostic Polarity (⚌ ⚎)

which is *within* Istence Reality

(pointing to this Polarity within Istence in Figure 2A, to these two

branches of Figure 3, then to these eight pairs of adjacent hexagrams of

the sixth ring of Figure 4 which have this (⚌ ⚎) fourth-fifth

and-sixth-line Yin-Yang configuration contrast).

Existence: Being's *universal* Form -

That which is Fathomable of Being.

Transexistence is *Void* of Being's Form -

That of Being which is Unknowable.

Antistence is Nonbeing's *primal* Void -

Of Nonbeing, the Unfathomable.

Istence is the *Form* of Nonbeing's Void -

That of Nonbeing which is Knowable. (Treon, 1989)

Of the ancient Yin-Yang circle symbol (see back cover of book),

Existential Reality is Yin (large black area)

and Transexistence is Yang *within* Yin (small white circle).

Antistential Reality is Yang (large white area)

and Istential Realm is Yin *within* Yang (small black circle). (Treon, 1989)

Typical of transcendent expression

this Tao of Onliness cosmology

brims over with *apparent* paradox.

When Spirit is seen through the mental eye

It seems, as Wilber says, a paradox. (Wilber, 1990)

Again, transcendent Realization

across and *as* all Knowingness Itself

from Perspective of One of these four Realms-

Antistence or Istence Realities;

Existence or Transexistential Realms-

is what Pan-gnostic means in this context.

Transcendental Trans-realization

as and *beyond* all Knowingness Itself

from Perspective of One of these four Realms

is what Trans-gnostic means in this context.

Sage, arising from and returning to

supreme Prim-istent Trans-gnostic Being (☰☰)

(pointing to this Reality in Figure 2A, to this branch of Figure 3, then

to the eight fourth-and-fifth-line (☰☰) fifth ring pentagrams of Figure 4):

Prim-ist *universive* Polarity

between *Trans-gnostic Transexistence* Realm (☰☰)

(pointing to this Consciousness Reality in Figure 2A, to this branch of

Figure 3, then to the eight fourth-fifth-and-sixth-line (☰☰) sixth

ring hexagrams of Figure 4)

and this *Pan-gnostic Transexistence* Realm (☰☰)

(pointing to this Reality in Figure 2A, to this branch of Figure 3, then

to the eight fourth-fifth-and-sixth-line (☰☰) sixth ring hexagrams of Figure 4).

This Trans- and Pan gnostic Polarity (☰☰ ☰☰)

within Transexistence Reality

(pointing to this Polarity within Transexistence in Figure 2A, to these

two branches of Figure 3, then to the eight pairs of adjacent

fourth-fifth-and-sixth-line (☰☰ ☰☰) sixth ring hexagrams of Figure 4).

Arising from and thence returning to

supreme Prim-istent Pan-gnostic Being (☰ ☰)

(pointing to this Consciousness Reality in Figure 2A, to this branch of

Figure 3, then to the eight fourth-and-fifth-line (☰ ☰) pentagrams of

the fifth ring of Figure 4):

Prim-ist *universive* Polarity

of *Trans-gnostic Existence* Consciousness (☰ ☰)

(pointing to this Realm in Figure 2A, to this branch of Figure 3, then to the eight fourth-fifth-and-sixth-line ($\equiv\!\equiv$) sixth ring hexagrams of Figure 4)

and *Pan-gnostic Existence* Consciousness ($\equiv\ \equiv$)

(pointing to this Realm in Figure 2A, to this branch of Figure 3, then to the eight fourth-fifth-and-sixth-line ($\equiv\ \equiv$) sixth ring hexagrams of Figure 4).

This Trans- and Pan- gnostic Polarity ($\equiv\!\equiv\ \ \equiv\ \equiv$)

within Existential Reality

(pointing to this Polarity within Existence in Figure 2A, to these two branches of Figure 3, then to the eight pairs of adjacent fourth-fifth-and-sixth-line ($\equiv\!\equiv\ \ \equiv\ \equiv$) sixth ring hexagrams of Figure 4).

Overhead drifter sees two white gulls

turning to sail with the wind,

silhouetted in the bright blue sky.

His face serene, mute looks on the lake.

Drifter returns to his diagrams.

Lo: There are two Prim-istent Polarities

    between Transexistence and Existence

    and two *between* Istence and Antistence:

    Prim-ist *universive* Polarity

    between *Trans-gnostic Transexistence* Realm ($\equiv\!\equiv$)

    (pointing to this Reality in Figure 2A, to this branch of Figure 3, then to the eight fourth-fifth-and-sixth-line ($\equiv\!\equiv$) sixth ring hexagrams of Figure 4)

    and *Pan-gnostic Existence* Consciousness ($\equiv\ \equiv$)

(pointing to this Realm in Figure 2A, to this branch of Figure 3, then to the eight fourth-fifth-and-sixth-line (☰ ☰) sixth ring hexagrams of Figure 4).

Prim-ist *universive* Polarity

of *Trans-gnostic Existence* Consciousness (☲ ☲)

(pointing to this Realm in Figure 2A, to this branch of Figure 3, then to these eight fourth-fifth-sixth-line (☲ ☲) sixth ring hexagrams of Figure 4)

and *Pan-gnostic Transexistential* Realm (☲)

(pointing to this Reality in Figure 2A, to this branch of Figure 3, then to these eight fourth-fifth-and-sixth-line (☲) sixth ring hexagrams of Figure 4).

Prim-ist *universive* Polarity

between *Pan-gnostic Istence* Consciousness (☳)

(pointing to this Realm in Figure 2A, to this branch of Figure 3, then to these eight fourth-fifth-and-sixth-line (☳) sixth ring hexagrams of Figure 4)

and *Trans-gnostic Antistence* Consciousness (☷)

(pointing to this Realm in Figure 2A, to this branch of Figure 3, then to these eight fourth-fifth-and-sixth-line (☷) sixth ring hexagrams of Figure 4)

Prim-ist *universive* Polarity

between *Trans-gnostic Istence* Consciousness (☶)

(pointing to this Realm in Figure 2A, to this branch of Figure 3, then to these eight fourth-fifth-and-sixth-line (☶) sixth ring hexagrams of Figure 4) and *Pan-gnostic Antistence* Consciousness (☰)

(pointing to this Realm in Figure 2A, to this branch of Figure 3, then to these eight fourth-fifth-and-sixth-line (☰) sixth ring hexagrams of Figure 4).

Mute gazes upon drifter's papers
spread out on the seat between them.
Learned one looks into the mute's face,
on which no expression can be seen.

A wind-gust picks up these diagrams
scattering them about the boat.
Drifter quickly gathers each paper,
placing it again upon the seat.
He weighs each down with a lead sinker
which he takes from his tackle box.
Lo: These four *universive* Polarities;

 two *between* Antistence and Existence,

 two *between* Istence and Transexistence:

Prim-ist *universive* Polarity
of *Trans-gnostic Antistence* Consciousness (☰)
(pointing to this Realm in Figure 2A, to this branch of Figure 3, then to these eight fourth-fifth-and-sixth-line (☰) sixth ring hexagrams of Figure 4)
and *Pan-gnostic Existence* Consciousness (☳)
(pointing to this Realm in Figure 2A, to this branch of Figure 3, then

to these eight fourth-fifth-and-sixth-line (☲ ☲) sixth ring hexagrams which, on this sixth ring, are directly opposite of each of the above (☰) hexagrams of Figure 4).

Prim-ist *universive* Polarity

of *Pan-gnostic Antistence* Consciousness (☷)

(pointing to this Realm in Figure 2A, to 'this branch of Figure 3, then to these eight fourth-fifth-and-sixth-line (☷) sixth ring hexagrams of Figure 4)

and *Trans-gnostic Existence* Consciousness (☵)

(pointing to this Realm in Figure 2A, to this branch of Figure 3, then to these eight fourth-fifth-and-sixth-line (☵) sixth ring hexagrams of Figure 4).

Prim-ist *universive* Polarity

between *Trans-gnostic Istence* Consciousness (☲)

(pointing to this Realm in Figure 2A, to this branch of Figure 3, then to these eight fourth-fifth-and-sixth line (☱) sixth ring hexagrams of Figure 4)

and *Pan-gnostic Transexistential* Realm (☳)

(pointing to this Reality in Figure 2A, to this branch of Figure 3, then to these eight fourth-fifth-and-sixth-line (☳) sixth ring hexagrams of Figure 4).

Prim-ist *universive* Polarity

between *Pan-gnostic Istence* Consciousness (☴)

(pointing to this Realm in Figure 2A, to this branch of Figure 3, then to these eight fourth-fifth-and-sixth-line (☴) sixth ring hexagrams of

Figure 4)

and *Trans-gnostic Transexistential* Realm (☰)

(pointing to this Reality in Figure 2A, to this branch of Figure 3, then to these eight fourth-fifth-and-sixth-line (☰) sixth ring hexagrams of Figure 4).

These eight *eternal universive* Realms

and their twelve transcendent Polarities.

I once thought that there were only four Realms: (Treon, 1989)

Istence and Antistence Realities,

plus Existence and Transexistence Realms.

I now see that *within Each* of These four

is *both* a Pan- and a Trans- gnostic Realm,

rather than Each as One *or* the Other.

Mute looks out on the sparkling lake

glistening in afternoon sunlight.

Drifter looks down at his diagrams.

Lo: Thus, arising from and returning to

these thirty-two *supreme* Prim-istent Realms

(his finger circles the thirty-two pentagrams of the fifth ring of Figure 4):

sixty-four Prim-ist *universive* Realms

(his finger circles the sixty-four hexagrams of the sixth ring of Figure 4);

also Their *ninety-six* Polarities.

These eight Polarized *universive* Realms:

two Existence Realms of *Apparency*,

two of Transexistence *Transparency*,

two *Parency* Istence Realities,

two Antistence of *Anti-parency*.

Early has turned to mid afternoon.

Still fishing, mute looks at passing clouds.

A stronger breeze begins to blow,

rippling sunlight on the lake.

Lo: We are Blooms of Pan-gnostic Existence.

Sage, for Us, this Realm is preeminent

(pointing to this Reality and to its three sub-Realities in Figure 2A,

then to the three innermost rings of Figure 4).

Our *way* is Pan-gnostic Existence,

this inner predisposing Point of View.

It is through these Manifest *only* Eyes

that we See Absolute Reality.

Transcending these Eyes in Enlightenment,

Centered in Prim-istence, of which It Is,

enfolded Pan-gnostic Existence Realm

is *Unmanifest* in Its Deep Structure,

but Surface Structure *can* be *Manifest*.

Abstracted from Its Prim-istential Ground,

only Its Surface Structure can be Known.

Still This is a *profound* transcendent Face!

Thus, this *Face* of Pan-gnostic Existence

(pointing to this Realm and to its three sub-Realms in Figure 2A, then to the three innermost rings of Figure 4),

which of Itself is *only* Manifest.

This *singular* Pan-gnostic Existence.

This first Pan-gnostic Existential ring

(pointing to this innermost Yin and Yang unigram ring of Figure 4):

fundamental Pan-gnostic Existence

(pointing to this sub-Realm of Figure 2A),

arises from and thence returns back to

Prim-istent Pan-gnostic Existence Realm

(pointing to this relationship in Figure 2A).

Sage, arising from and returning to

universive Pan-gnostic Existence

(pointing to this Prim-istent Realm in Figure 2A)

is the *fundamental* Polarity

of *singular* Pan-gnostic Existence

between *form* of reflexive awareness (– –)

(pointing to this Yin (– –) unigram at the center of Figure 4, to

this branch of Figure 3, then to this Realm in Figure 2A),

and *void* unreflexive experience (——)

(pointing to this Yang (——) unigram at the center of Figure 4, to this

branch of Figure 3, then to this Realm in Figure 2A).

Fundamental Pan-gnostic Existence

(pointing to this sub-Reality in Figure 2A).

This configurative *productive form*

of Yin (‑ ‑) *awareness* reflexivity:

vision of *transparent apparency*.

This is awareness' *mind-psyche* Realm.

Awareness *mind-psyche omniscience*.

This transfigurative *creative void*

of unreflexive Yang (——) *experience*:

power of *apparent transparency*.

This is experience's *heart-soul* Realm.

Experience *heart-soul omnipotence*.

A heron flies slowly overhead.

It swoops down and gathers up a fish,

then flies off toward the distant shore.

Drifter watches it as if spellbound.

Mute scoops up lake water in his hand

and splashes it into drifter's face.

Startled, drifter stares at mute, then laughs.

Mute grins and points to drifter's papers,

upon which more water has been splashed.

Again, drifter sweeps the water off,

then dabs these dry with his handkerchief.

Learned one looks at his diagrams.

Lo: This second Pan-gnostic Existence ring

    (his finger circles the four Yin-Yang digrams of the second ring of Figure 4)

      called *cardinal* Pan-gnostic Existence

(pointing to this sub-Realm in Figure 2A).

It arises from and returns back to

fundamental Pan-gnostic Existence

(pointing to this relationship in Figure 2A).

There exist two *least* profound *cardinal*

Pan-gnostic Existence Polarities:

Arising from and thence returning to

this Yang (—) *experience* Reality

(pointing to this Consciousness Realm in Figures 2A, 3, and 4)

is greater cardinal *communion* Realm (⚌)

(pointing to this Reality in Figure 2A, to this branch of Figure 3, then

to this greater Hsiang (⚌) of the second ring of Figure 4),

and this lesser cardinal *compassion* Realm (⚍)

(pointing to this Reality in Figure 2A, to this branch of Figure 3, then

to this lesser Hsiang (⚍) of the second ring of Figure 4).

communion-compassion Polarity.

This Polarity of *experience*.

From *awareness* (- -) arises and returns

(pointing to this Realm in Figures 2A, 3, and 4)

this greater cardinal Realm of *meaning* (= =)

(pointing to this Reality in Figure 2A, to this branch of Figure 3, then

to this greater Hsiang (= =) of the second ring of Figure 4),

and this lesser cardinal *knowledge* Realm (⚎)

(pointing to this Reality in Figure 2A, to this branch of Figure 3, then to this lesser Hsiang (⚎) of the second ring of Figure 4).

Polarity of meaning and knowledge.

This Polarity of *awareness* Realm.

Sage, there are two *most* profound *cardinal*

Pan-gnostic Existence Polarities:

This *greater* cardinal Polarity

of transcendent *meaning* (⚏) and *communion* (⚌)

(pointing to these Realms in Figure 2A, to these branches of Figure 3,

then to these two greater Hsiang (⚏ ⚌) digrams of the second

ring of Figure 4),

and *lesser* cardinal Polarity

of transcendent *knowledge* (⚎) and *compassion* (⚍)

(pointing to these Realms in Figure 2A, to these branches of Figure 3,

then to these two lesser Hsiang (⚎ ⚍) digrams of the second

ring of Figure 4).

Four *cardinal* Realms, four Polarities:

between *communion* (⚌) and *compassion* (⚍) Realms,

of *meaning* (⚏) and *knowledge* (⚎) Realities;

also of *meaning* (⚏) and *communion* (⚌)

and between *knowledge* (⚎) and *compassion* (⚍) Realms

(pointing to these Polarities in Figure 2A and in the second ring of

Figure 4).

Of the ancient Yin-Yang circle symbol (see back cover of book),

the transcendent Realm of *meaning* is *Yin* (large black area) and *knowledge's* Realm is Yang *within* Yin (small white area).

The transcendent *communion* Realm is *Yang* (large white area)

and *compassion's* Realm is Yin *within* Yang (small black area).

These four Realms, indeed each and every Realm,

of singular Pan-gnostic Existence

are *trans-mental* in Realization.

Thus trans-symbolic and trans-rational.

Yet of Their mental surface one may speak,

if only in this superficial way.

Sage, *no* mutual exclusion occurs

in the Way that is Tao of Onliness.

On the Surface one Path predominates,

but at Its Deep Source all Paths equal It.

At Deep Source No-distinction can be made,

at Deep Source there *are* no separate Paths.

Awakened *source of oneness* communion:

serene and *transparent* infusive bliss.

This is communion's *heart* Reality.

This *communion heart* of *omnipotence*.

Resonance of *luminous* compassion:

righteous and *holy* inspired presence.

This is compassion's *soul* Reality.

This *compassion soul* of *omnipotence*.

Meanings *fertile conceptive* genesis:

inherency and *multiplicity*.

Sage, this is meaning's *mind* Reality.

This is *meaning's mind* of *omniscience*.

Silent comprehending knowledge psyche:

intuitive, realizative Realm.

This is the Realm of knowledge's *psyche*.

This *knowledge psyche* of *omniscience*.

Mute is resoundingly flatulent.

Drifter fans the air and turns away.

Mute looks at learned one and smiles.

Soon both rock the boat with laughter.

Mute drops his line into the lake.

Soon he pulls out yet another fish.

Learned one watches him for a time,

then looks out across the blue water.

Drifter looks down at his diagrams.

Lo: This third Pan-gnostic Existential ring

     (his finger circles the eight Yin-Yang trigrams of the third ring of Figure 4):

     elemental Pan-gnostic Existence

     (pointing to this sub-Realm of Figure 2A).

It arises from and returns back to

cardinal Pan-gnostic Existence Realm

(pointing to this relationship in Figure 2A).

There are four *least* profound *elemental*

Pan-gnostic Existence Polarities:

From *communion* arises and returns

this Polarity, called *elemental*,

of *serenity* (⚏) and *transparency* (☰)

(pointing to these Realms in Figure 2A, to these branches of Figure 3,

then to these two trigrams of the third ring of Figure 4).

From *compassion* arises and returns

this *elemental* Polarization

between *righteousness* (☳) and *holiness* (☶) Realms

(pointing to these Consciousness Realities in Figure 2A, to these

branches of Figure 3, then to these two trigrams of the third ring of

Figure 4).

Arising from, returning to *knowledge*

is this *elemental* Polarity:

realization (☱) and *intuition* (☴)

(pointing to these Realms of Figure 2A, to these branches of Figure 3,

then to these two trigrams of the third ring of Figure 4).

Arising from, returning to *meaning*

is this *elemental* Polarity:

inherency (☰☷) and *multiplicity* (☷ ☷)

(pointing to these Realms in Figure 2A, to these branches of Figure 3, then to these two trigrams of the third ring of Figure 4).

There are four *more* profound *elemental*

Pan-gnostic Existence Polarities:

between *transparency* (☰) and *holiness* (☶)

(pointing to these Realities in Figure 2A, to these branches of Figure 3, then to these two trigrams of the third ring of Figure 4),

between *serenity* (☵) and *righteousness* (☱)

(pointing to these two Realms in Figures 2A, 3, and 4 in the way described above),

of *intuition* (☳) - *multiplicity* (☷ ☷)

(pointing to these two Realms in figures 2A, 3, and 4 in the way described above),

of *realization* (☴) - *inherency* (☰☷)

(pointing to these two Realms in Figures 2A, 3, and 4 in the way described above).

There are four *most* profound *elemental*

Pan-gnostic Existence Polarities:

of *transparency* (☰) and *inherency* (☰☷),

of *serenity* (☵) - *multiplicity* (☷ ☷),

between *righteousness* (☱) and *intuition* (☳),

of *holiness* (☶) and *realization* (☴)

(respectively pointing to these Realms in Figure 2A, to these directly
opposite branches of Figure 3, then to these directly opposite trigrams
of the third ring of Figure 4).

Thus, twelve *elemental* Polarities
of eight *elemental* Realities
of Pan-gnostic Existence's third ring
(his finger circles the third ring of Figure 4).

Pan-gnostic Existence *transparency*:
Homeward Voyager's none all-where *of-ness*;
communion's void, emptiness of worlds.
One comes to See Yin Actlessness (☶), Yang Am (☰)
only through transcendent *transparency* (☰)
(pointing to this relationship and derivation in Figure 4).

Pan-gnostic Existence *serenity*:
Profound Sage's one all-where *unity*;
communion's form, foundation of worlds.
One Sees Yin Emptiness (☷), Yang Radiance (☳)
only through transcendent *serenity* (☷)
(pointing to this relationship and derivation in Figure 4).

The boat rocks gently with the waves.
These two men rock thusly to and fro.
Mute looks down into the clear water.

Drifter continues his monologue.

Lo: Pan-gnostic Existence *inherency*:

Concealed Sage's one each-where *in-ness*;

meaning's void, hidden wellspring of worlds.

One comes to See Yin Am (☵), Yang Actlessness (☴)

only through transcendent *inherency* (☷)

(pointing to this relationship and derivation in Figure 4).

This elemental *multiplicity*:

reflection's none each-where *fertility*;

meaning's form, illuminated worlds.

One Sees Yin Radiance (☶), Yang Emptiness (☴)

through this transcendent *multiplicity* (☷)

(pointing to this relationship and derivation in Figure 4).

Lake gulls swoop and cry out overhead

searching for their afternoon meal.

Mute pulls in a bright yellow sunfish,

unhooks it and puts it in the cage.

Drifter looks into the lake's green depths,

through the water's great clarity.

Mute baits his hook, tosses out his line.

Learned one leans over his papers.

Lo: Pan-gnostic Existential *righteousness*:

love's consuming each each-where *with-ness* flame;

compassion's void, this fire of worlds.

One comes to See Yin Mind (☵), Yang Onliness (☴)

only through transcendental *righteousness* (⚏)

(pointing to this relationship and derivation in Figure 4).

Pan-gnostic Existential *holiness*:

each all-where *luminosity* of love;

compassion's form, this body of worlds.

Yin Awakening (☳) and Yang Mystery (☴),

Seen only through transcendent *holiness* (⚎)

(pointing to this relationship and derivation in Figure 4)

Mute puts his pole inside the boat

and closes his beat-up tackle box.

Learned one briefly looks up at him

and then returns to his diagrams.

Mute pulls up and looks at the fish cage.

Fish frantically twist and flap about

splashing water onto both of them.

Mute returns the cage to the water.

Drifter sweeps water from his papers.

He looks into the mute's smiling eyes,

then he too smiles with the mute.

Learned one returns to his papers.

Lo: Pan-gnostic Existence *intuition*:

Great Voyager's all all-where *through-ness* Realm;

knowledge's void, creator of worlds.

One comes to See Yin Onliness (☳), Yang Mind (☴)

only though transcendent *intuition* (☲)

(pointing to this relationship and derivation in Figure 4).

This elemental *realization*:

psyche's beacon, all each-where *clarity*;

knowledge's form, trans-essence of worlds.

Yin Mystery (☵) and Yang Awakening (☳),

Seen through transcendent *realization* (☲)

(pointing to this relationship and derivation in Figure 4).

All Beings are of *one* Buddha-nature.

All Beings are Christ-consciousness *Itself*.

Thus all Beings *equally* and *fully*

share deep-structure potential and access

to each and every Level, Realm, and Stage

of Tao of Onliness cosmology.

Only in manifest surface-structures

here described in Levels, Realms, and Stages

of Tao of Onliness cosmology

do Beings differ in *degree* to which

each *tends* to express these different Realms.

Mute pulls the anchor into the boat

while drifter folds his diagrams

and put them into his pocket.

Learned one rows the boat to shore.

Both get out and pull it onto land.

Drifter takes a knife from his backpack,
then walks the cage to a nearby stump.
Cutting off their heads and tails,
he scales and cleans eight pan fish.
He leaves these remains for the raccoons.

Mute gathers wood among the trees
and brings it to the sandy beach.
He piles it and lights a fire.

The two seat themselves before the flame.
Drifter removes foil from his pack
and with it wraps each of the eight fish.
He sets these fish on a nearby rock,
then takes two potatoes from the pack.
He wraps these tightly with the foil
and drops them into the fire.

Mid has turned to late afternoon.
Pine trees cast long shadows on the lake.
The warm campfire cracks and sparks.
Scent of burning wood now fills the air.

They sit before the flame in silence.
Learned one gazes at the fire.

Smoking his pipe, mute looks on the lake.

Lo: With I Ching, We look deeply into Self;

   We See the Face of Self Reality.

   Through I Ching We can See transcendent Realms

   and Know the Way of Consciousness Itself.

   We are I Ching and It is Us also;

   Revelations of Nonduality.

   Sage, through I Ching Insight and Mindfulness

   We See into Our Buddha-nature.

Mute lies back upon the sandy beach.

Drifter looks into the dancing flame.

Above, wind whispers in the pines.

Learned one adds wood to the fire,

then puts the wrapped fish into the flame.

Bird songs come from the woods behind them.

A gentle breeze blows in from the lake.

Lo: I Ching is not a carnival side-show.

   I Ching is not a fortune teller game.

   I Ching is a Way of meditation,

   an *early-stage* Path of contemplation.

   Through I Ching We can transcend space-time realm

   and See the Source from which space-time evolves.

   Sage, I Ching *indirectly* Views space-time

   from the Foundation of its Origins.

   It Views the *broad direction* of space-time.

   Thus, It Sees deeply into space-time realm,

but *cannot* predict futures of space-time.

I Ching is of transcendent Knowledge Realm.

This Knowledge Realm cannot validly judge

empiric physical space-time knowledge,

or vice versa, as Wilber indicates. (Wilber, 1990)

Mute sits up and looks at learned one.

He removes his tattered canvas shoes,

rolls up his pants and walks to the lake.

He wades in and strolls along the shore.

Soon drifter joins him in the water.

Slowly they walk about in silence,

feeling the sand beneath their feet

and warm lake water on their legs;

watching sunlight dance upon the lake.

Mute splashes water onto drifter.

Drifter quickly returns the splash.

They duck and jump, splashing each other,

laughing and howling as they play.

Soon they sit drying before the flame.

When he is dry, drifter gets a stick

and pulls the potatoes from the flame.

In this same way he removes the fish.

From the backpack of the learned one

mute removes a thermos, two hard rolls,

pepper, spread, a lemon, and two forks.

Unwrapping the fish and potatoes,

they season these and feast upon them,

drinking water from the thermos jar.

After eating, they clean up their mess.

The sun is low and about to set.

Drifter adds wood to the fire.

A loon crys out from across the lake.

These two figures sit in solitude.

Lo: Let me describe this I Ching *supplement*

that I call Tao of Onliness I Ching.

It is a *minor complement* to text,

symbol, and commentary of I Ching.

This metaphoric abstract Onliness

is but *one* way of Knowing the I Ching;

merely *one* Interpretation of It.

Yet Its inherency is here Expressed.

Tao of Onliness springs from the I Ching

but alters *nothing* of I Ching Itself.

It is an I Ching transcendent Vision,

but through, in, with, and of I Ching Itself.

Sage, in this Tao of Onliness I Ching

is presented *image, text, expression*

for *each* hexagram of the Book of Change

from Perspective of Tao of Onliness.

The *images* are photos that I take,

assigning each one to a hexagram

through consultation with the Book of Change.

The *texts* have been selected in this way:

Two Sages provide many of the *texts*;

You (pointing to the mute), and the Awakened recluse woman.

I have selected the remaining ones

from transcendent Writings of the world.

Such Writings as *directly* Speak to Me.

All *texts* have been assigned to hexagrams

through consultation with the Book of Change.

Each *expression* of this Cosmology,

as Manifested in each hexagram,

evolves through consultation with I Ching.

It is now twilight, nearly dark.

Firelight flickers in the cove.

Drifter and mute look upon the flame.

In silence, they sit into nightfall.

Mute stands up, stretches, then walks about.

He puts more wood upon the fire.

Mute watches as the fire grows,

then turns and walks away from it.

Suddenly he turns back, starts running,

and jumps feet-first into the flame.

A blinding fiery explosion

engulfs this whole reality.

Mute, drifter, shore, cove, trees, lake, and sky—

all of this reality consumed.

The flame alone is and remains.

Slowly it too fades and is no more.

Neither Apparency Appears

nor does Transparency Transpear.

Nor does Istential Parency Pear.

Existence, Transexistence, Istence;

all are transcended *Totally*.

Antistential Anti-parency

unutterably Anti-pears.

Identity lost unto Itself,

and even lostness Anti-pears.

Only Anti-pearingness "remains".

CHAPTER THREE

The Flower of Prim-holistent Am

III

"*Seeing the Ox.* The boy finds the way by the sound he hears; he sees thereby into the origin of things, and all his senses are in harmonious order. In all his activities, it is manifestly present. It is like the salt in water and the glue in colour. [It is there though not distinguishable as an individual entity.] When the eye is properly directed, he will find that it is no other than himself.
    On a yonder branch perches a nightingale cheerfully
        singing;
    The sun is warm, and a soothing breeze blows, on the
        bank the willows are green;
    The ox is there all by himself, nowhere is he to hide
        himself;
    The splendid head decorated with stately horns—what
        painter can reproduce him?"

-from "The Ten Oxherding Pictures"
by Kaku-an
-compiled by D. T. Suzuki
from *Manual of Zen Buddhism*

"At the subtle level, this process of "interiorization" . . .
intensifies—a new transcendence with a new depth, a
new embrace, a higher consciousness, a wider identity . . .
which discloses at its summit a divine union of Soul and
Spirit, a union *prior* to any of its manifestations as matter
or life or mind, . . . and the God within announces itself in
terms undreamt of in gross manifestation, with a Light that
blinds the sun . . . —that Spirit is intuited at the psychic
and comes to the fore in the subtle stage of consciousness evolution, utterly including the previous stages,
utterly outshining them. Let the Earth and Cosmos and
World dissolve, and see Spirit still shining in the Emptiness, never arising, never dissolving . . . "

                          -Ken Wilber
                          from *Sex, Ecology, Spirituality:*
                          The Spirit of Evolution
                          (see Appendix C)

Through wild flowers and tall grasses
high atop a towering mountain
walk two figures toward its summit.

Recluse woman and learned man
reach the summit of the mountain
and look out on its distant vistas
They see a crystal tropic morning
and feel trade winds gently blowing.
All around them in the distance
lies the blue majestic ocean.
Just below are mountain canyons
spreading down and out before them.
Beyond these lie green rolling foothills
and the island's rocky sea cliffs
with scattered sandy palm-lined beaches.

In solitude of tropic splendor

at the summit of the mountain

in a shaded cove together

sit recluse and the learned drifter.

For a long time they are silent

gazing at the windblown grasses

and the distant sun-streaked ocean.

Recluse: In egoic darkness,

        your life passes like this gust of wind

        swirling and dissipating

        in eddies round about.

        You are Eternity Itself and Know It not.

Learned one looks over at her.

Without expression she looks forward.

Lo: It's true, I wander in egoic night

    and with me drag this Tao of Onliness.

    In this way I am blind to much of It.

    Yet the world's pleasures, my desires,

    are less and less interesting to me.

    My attachment to these becomes weaker.

    As this occurred, I thought I must be mad

    but now See that I am becoming sane.

Once again silence rests between them.

Both look out upon the distant sea.

Drifter takes two papers from his pack

and puts these on the ground before them.

Lo: Sage, this is *Tao Of Am* Polarity (pointing to Figure 5).

   This Flower of Primal Holistent *Am* (continuing to point to Figure 5)

   from Perspective of Tao of Onliness

   as Seen through Pan-gnostic Existent eyes.

   I speak of Tao of Onliness I Ching

   and Its flowering *Am* Polarity

   (pointing to the fourth-ring Yin and Yang Am quadrigrams of Figure 4).

   Two Prim-holistential *absolute* Realms

   in Prim-ist *absolute* Polarity.

Drifter looks out at the distant shore.

Recluse looks upon the vast ocean

stretching out as far as eye can see.

Drifter returns to his diagrams.

Lo: Self of *Yang Am* Enlightenment (☰);

   Self of *Yin Am* Enlightenment (☷)

   are the Names of These *absolute* Am Realms

   here fused in *absolute* Polarity

   (respectively pointing to these two innermost quadrigrams of Figure 5).

   Though Am's Deep Structure is Unmanifest,

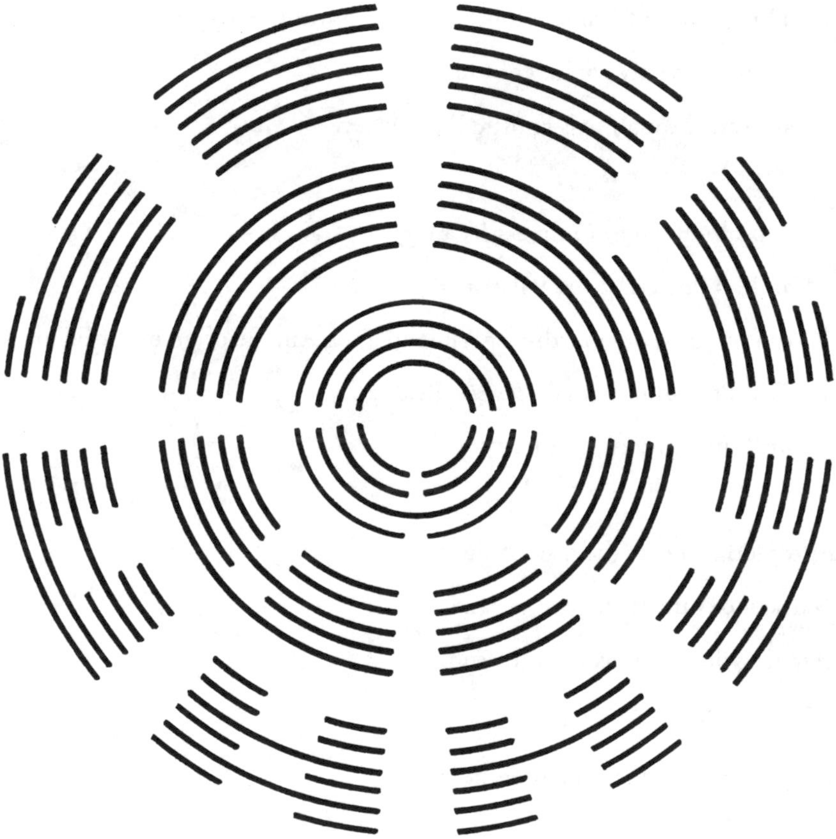

Figure 5

Am's Yin-Yang Surface *can* be Manifest.

Each Realm is a Path of Enlightenment

conjoined in *absolute* Polarity

(pointing to the Yin and Yang Am (⚏ ☰) Realms in Figure 4).

Each Merges with the Other fifteen Paths

(his finger circles the sixteen fourth-ring quadrigrams of Figure 4)

Emerging as Enlightenment Only...

This *Self* of Unconditionality.

This Trans-istential Trans-manifested

Consciousness Itself without a second.

Recluse stretches out on the warm ground,

resting her head on a tuft of grass.

Drifter looks intently at her face.

She smiles and pulls upon his leg.

Drifter nods knowingly and smiles.

Putting the large diagram away (Figure 4),

drifter takes out his photo album.

He turns to the paper on the ground.

Lo: Freely arising from, returning to

     Self of Yang Am Enlightenment's *absolute* Reality (☰)

     (pointing to this quadrigram in Figure 5)

     are two *supreme* Realities of Am:

     Self of Trans-gnostic Nonbeing Am (☰)

and Self of Pan-gnostic Nonbeing Am (☷)

(pointing respectively to these two second-ring pentagrams in Figure 5).

Likewise arising from, returning to

Self of Yin Am Enlightenment's *absolute* Reality (☵)

(pointing to this quadrigram in Figure 5)

are two remaining *supreme* Realms of Am:

Self of Pan-gnostic Being Am (☳)

in greater *supreme* Polarity with

Self of Trans-gnostic Nonbeing Am (☶)

(pointing respectively to these two second-ring pentagrams in Figure 5),

and Self of Trans-gnostic Being Am (☴)

in lesser *supreme* Polarity with

Self of Pan-gnostic Nonbeing Am (☷)

(pointing respectively to these two second-ring pentagrams in Figure 5).

Birthless, deathless Being and Nonbeing,

This Ultimate *supreme* Polarity.

Realities of Being's boundless *Bliss*

and Realms of Nonbeing's boundless *Freedom*. (Treon, 1989)

Realms of *supreme* Being's *Holomorphosis*,

supreme Nonbeing's *Hologenesis*.

The Beauty of Being's infinite *Form*,

the infinite *Void* of Nonbeingness.

The *Unspeakable Grandeur* of Being,

the *Awesome Mystery* of Nonbeing.

Each by the Other founded and sustained,

Each within Other seeded and contained.

In the tree above them songbirds sing.

Recluse is asleep upon the ground.

Drifter looks upon her in repose

and then returns to his diagram.

Lo: In turn arising from, returning to

supreme Realm's Self of Trans-gnostic Nonbeing Am (☰)

are these two *universive* Realms of Am,

two of sixty-four I Ching hexagrams:

First, this *first* hexagram of the I Ching

In Tao of Onliness I Ching it's called

Numinous Revelation Self of *Am*

(pointing to this hexagram in Figure 5):

(*Numinous Revelation* Self of *Am*)

Here is the *image* of this hexagram

(pointing to a photo in his album) (Photo #1),

and these words are its profound Voice or *text*:

"One day Tokusan was sitting outside

trying to look into the mystery of Zen.

Ryutan said, 'Why don't you come in?'

Replied Tokusan, 'It is pitch dark.'

A candle was lighted and held out to Tokusan.

When he was at the point of taking it

Ryutan suddenly blew out the light,

whereupon the mind of Tokusan was opened."

-from *An Introduction to Zen Buddhism*

by D. T. Suzuki

This, its Tao of Onliness *expression*:

In singular Pan-gnostic Existence;

Am experience's *genesis* of *Creativity*

Am communion's *heart* of *Genesis*

Am transparency: Empty Sage's *heart* of *transfigurative Origin*

Expressed in Prim-istent Reality,

it is *Numinous Revelation* Self of *Trans-gnostic Antistential Am*.

This *Numinous Revelation* Self of *Am* Reality (☰)

(pointing to this third-ring hexagram in Figure 5).

Second, I Ching's *forty-third* hexagram.

In Tao of Onliness I Ching it's called

Infinite Uncontracted Self of *Am*

(pointing to this hexagram in Figure 5):

(*Infinite Uncontracted* Self of *Am*)

Here is the *image* of this hexagram

(pointing to a photo in his album) (Photo #?),

and these words its initial Voice or *text*:

> "I am the light that is over all things.
>
> I am all:
>
> all came forth from me,
>
> and all attained to me.
>
> Split a piece of wood,
>
> and I am there.
>
> Pick up a stone,
>
> and you will find me there."
>
> -Jesus (The Gospel of Thomas
>
> *The Secret Teaching of Jesus*

and these words, its completed Voice or *text*:

> "And the angel of the LORD appeared unto him
>
> in a flame of fire out of the midst of a bush:
>
> and he looked, and, behold, the bush burned with fire,

and the bush *was* not consumed.

And Moses said, I will now turn aside,

and see this great sight,

why the bush is not burnt.

And when the LORD saw that he turned aside to see,

God called unto him out of the midst of the bush,

and said, Moses, Moses. And he said, Here *am* I.

And he said, Draw not nigh hither:

put off thy shoes from off thy feet,

for the place whereon thou standest *is* holy ground. . .

And Moses said unto God, Behold,

when I come unto the children of Israel, and shall say unto them,

The God of your fathers hath sent me unto you,

and they shall say to me, what is his name?

what shall I say unto them?

And God said unto Moses, I AM THAT I AM:

and he said, Thus shalt thou say unto the children of Israel,

I AM hath sent me unto you."

- The Holy Bible (King James

Version) Exodus, Chapter Three

Verses 2, 3, 4, 5, 13, and 14

This, its Tao of Onliness *expression*:

In singular Pan-gnostic Existence;

Am experience's Numinous *apparent transparency*

Am communion's trans-mental *Origin heart*

Am transparency's *heart* of *none all-where Potency*

Expressed in Prim-istent Reality,

it is *Infinite Uncontracted* Self of *Pan-gnostic Antistential Am.*

This *Infinite Uncontracted* Self of *Am* Reality (☰)

(pointing to this third-ring hexagram in Figure 5).

Drifter looks at recluse who still sleeps.

Turning, he looks out upon the sea.

Tall grasses rustle in the wind.

Scent of wild flowers fill the air.

Drifter stands and walks about the peak.

His pants and shirt flap in the strong wind

and his beard and hair toss to and fro.

He walks slowly, stopping now and then

to look out upon majestic views

of lush canyons, rocky cliffs and sea.

Drifter returns to the grassy cove

lined with a vertical gray rock wall,

very near to the mountain's summit.

Full-lotus, facing this rock wall,

he sits zazen and meditates.

Recluse soon awakens and sits up.

She stands up, stretches and looks about,

and then walks to the mountain's peak.

She sits facing North and meditates.

Her hair streams and tosses in the wind.

In about an hour she returns

and sits down beside the drifter.

He is looking at his diagram.

Lo: Likewise arising from, returning to

supreme Realm's Self of Pan-gnostic Being Am (☷)

are two more *universive* Realms of Am:

First, this *fifteenth* hexagram of I Ching.

In Tao of Onliness I Ching it's called

Unqualifiable Self of *Am*

(pointing to this hexagram in Figure 5):

(*Unqualifiable* Self of *Am*)

Here is the *image* of this hexagram

(pointing to a photo in his album) (Photo #3),

and these words are its profound Voice or *text*:

"All Buddhas and all ordinary beings are nothing but

the one mind. The mind is beginningless and endless, unborn and indestructible. It has no color or shape, neither exists nor doesn't exist, isn't old or new, long or short, large or small, since it transcends all measures, limits, names, and comparisons. It is what you see in front of you. Start to think about it and immediately you are mistaken. It is like the boundless void, which can't be fathomed or measured. The one mind is the Buddha, and there is no distinction between Buddha and ordinary beings, except that ordinary beings are attached to forms and thus seek Buddhahood outside themselves. . . They don't know that all they have to do is put a stop to conceptual thinking, and the Buddha will appear before them, because this mind is the Buddha and Buddha is all living beings."

- Huang-Po

The Enlightened Mind

This, its Tao of Onliness *expression*:
In singular Pan-gnostic Existence;
Am awareness' *morphosis* of *Productivity*
in *fundamental* Polarity with
Am experience's *genesis* of *Creativity*
Am meaning's *mind* of *Morphosis*
fused in *cardinal* Polarity with
Am communion's *heart* of *Genesis*
Am inherency: Concealed Sage's *mind* of *configurative Source*

in *elemental* Polarity with

Am transparency: Empty Sage's *heart* of *transfigurative Origin*

Expressed in Prim-istent Reality,

it is *Unqualifiable* Self of *Pan-gnostic Existential Am*,

this *Unqualifiable* Self of *Am* Reality (☶),

fused in *universive* Polarity

with *Numinous Revelation* Self of *Trans-gnostic Antistential Am* (☰)

(pointing respectively to these two third-ring hexagrams in Figure 5).

Next, I Ching's *fifty-second* hexagram.

In Tao of Onliness I Ching it's called

Unsurpassable Transfinite Self of *Am*

(pointing to this hexagram in Figure 5):

(*Unsurpassable Transfinite* Self of *Am*)

Here is the *image* of this hexagram

(pointing to a photo in his album) (Photo #4),

and these words are its profound Voice or *text*:

"Ryokan, a Zen master, lived the simplest kind of life

in a little hut at the foot of a mountain.

One evening a thief visited the hut

only to discover there was nothing in it to steal.

Ryokan returned and caught him.

'You may have come a long way to visit me,' he told the prowler,

'and you should not return empty-handed.

Please take my clothes as a gift.'

The thief was bewildered. He took the clothes and slunk away.

Ryokan sat naked, watching the moon.

'Poor fellow,' he mused,

'I wish I could give him this beautiful moon.' "

-from *Zen Flesh, Zen Bones*

compiled by Paul Reps

This, its Tao of Onliness *expression*:

In singular Pan-gnostic Existence;

Am awareness' Numinous *transparent apparency*

in *fundamental* Polarity with

Am experience's Numinous *apparent transparency*

Am meaning's trans-mental *Vortex mind*

fused in *cardinal* Polarity with

Am communion's trans-mental *Origin heart*

Am inherency's *mind* of *one each-where Ubiquity*

in *elemental* Polarity with

Am transparency's *heart* of *none all-where Potency*

Expressed in Prim-istent Reality,

it is *Unsurpassable Transfinite* Self of *Trans-gnostic Existential Am,*

this *Unsurpassable Transfinite* Self of *Am* Reality (☲),

fused in *universive* Polarity

with *Infinite Uncontracted* Self of *Pan-gnostic Antistential Am* (☰)

(pointing respectively to these two third-ring hexagrams in Figure 5).

Late morning has turned to afternoon.

Warm sunshine blankets the mountain top.

Above, birds float upon the wind.

The two sit looking out to sea.

Recluse gets up and walks about.

Yawning, she stretches in the sunlight.

Drifter lies back upon the grass

and watches as birds fly high above.

Recluse disappears in the tall grass,

and in a few moments she returns.

Learned one lies with his eyes closed,

napping in the shaded grassy cove

atop a tropic mountain island

set like a green jewel in blue sea.

Recluse sits down next to the drifter.

She looks on the distant breaking surf,

then upon the glistening blue sea.

The wind gusts, leaves rustle in the tree.

Drifter stirs and opens up his eyes.

He sees clouds pass on a sea of wind.

Drifter rolls over in the grass,

then sits up and views the distant shore

and great breakers crashing on the rocks.

Drifter returns to his diagram.

Lo: In turn arising from, returning to

    supreme Realm's Self of Pan-gnostic Nonbeing Am (☰)

    are these two *universive* Realms of Am:

    First, this *fourteenth* hexagram of I Ching.

    In Tao of Onliness I Ching it's called

    All-embracing Only Self of *Am*

    (pointing to this hexagram in Figure 5):

(*All-embracing Only* Self of *Am*)

    Here is the *image* of this hexagram

    (pointing to a photo in his album) (Photo #5),

    and these words are its profound Voice or *text*:

"We join spokes together in the wheel,

but it is the center hole

that makes the wagon move.

We shape clay into a pot,

but it is the emptiness inside

that holds whatever we want.

We hammer wood for a house,

but it is the inner space

that makes it livable.

We work with being,

but non-being is what we use."

- Lao-tzu from *Tao Te Ching*

Stephen Mitchell Translation

This, its Tao of Onliness *expression*:

In singular Pan-gnostic Existence;

Am experience's trans-symbolic *transfigurative* Self

Am communion's *Meditative heart*

Am transparency's *eternal Apprehending heart*

Expressed in Prim-istent Reality,

it is *All-embracing Only* Self of *Trans-gnostic Istential Am.*

This *All-embracing Only* Self of *Am* Reality (☰)

(pointing to this third-ring hexagram in Figure 5).

Second, I Ching's *thirty-fourth* hexagram.

In Tao of Onliness I Ching it's called

No-otherness Trans-istential Self of *Am*

(pointing to this hexagram in Figure 5):

(*No-otherness Trans-istential* Self of *Am*)

Here is the *image* of this hexagram

(pointing to a photo in his album) (Photo #6),

and these words are its profound Voice or *text*:

"The Atman (Absolute Self) is one, absolute, indivisible.

It is pure consciousness.

To imagine many forms within it

is like imagining palaces in the air.

Therefore, know that you are the Atman,

ever-blissful, one without a second,

and find ultimate peace."

- Shankara

from *The Enlightened Mind*

This, its Tao of Onliness *expression*:

In singular Pan-gnostic Existence;

Am experience's *unconditional Gnostic heart-soul*

Am communion's *peaceful Infusive heart*

Am transparency's *heart* of *Of-ness unreflexivity*

Expressed in Prim-istent Reality,

it is *No-otherness Tras-istential* Self of *Pan-gnostic Istential Am.*

This *No-otherness Trans-istential* Self of *Am* Reality (☰)

(pointing to this third-ring hexagram in Figure 5).

Trade winds increase and more clouds appear.

Drifter sits so as to face recluse.

Opening his backpack he removes

two oranges, jar of apple juice,

peanuts, dates, and sandwiches of cheese.

They eat lunch in quiet solitude

sharing this nourishing repast.

After lunch recluse finds a spot

to rest upon in the knee-high grass.

Soon drifter joins her and they nap.

In this grassy shelter they repose

sleeping into mid afternoon.

Learned one awakens and sits up.

He looks out across the sea of grass

and hears its soft whisper in the wind.

Recluse's eyes open, she sits up.

A hawk is circling high above.

Nearby, birds are chirping round about.

Far below, waves break on distant shores.

The two walk back to their sheltered cove

and sit down next to one another.

Recluse woman sits with her eyes closed.

Learned one spreads out his diagram.

Lo: Freely emerging from, returning to

   supreme Realm's Self of Trans-gnostic Being Am (☶)

   are these two *universive* Realms of Am:

First, this *thirty-ninth* I Ching hexagram.

In Tao of Onliness I Ching it's called

Non-striving, Non-resisting Self of *Am*

(pointing to this hexagram in Figure 5):

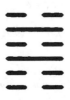

(*Non-striving, Non-resisting* Self of *Am*)

Here is the *image* of this hexagram

(pointing to a photo in his album) (Photo #7),

and Your words are its profound Voice or *text*:

> "Quester of Enlightenment,
>
> You are *already* That of which you seek.
>
> Your Searching is the *way* that you avoid,
>
> creating searcher and searched for duality.
>
> This is conditioned and conditional knowledge.
>
> Clinging self-possessive action dreams."
>
> - Recluse Sage

This, its Tao of Onliness *expression*:

In singular Pan-gnostic Existence;

Am awareness' trans-symbolic *configuration* Self

in *fundamental* Polarity with

Am experience's trans-symbolic *transfigurative* Self

Am meaning's *Insightful mind*

fused in *cardinal* Polarity with

Am communion's *Meditative heart*

Am inherency's *seminal Comprehending mind*

in *elemental* Polarity with

Am transparency's *eternal Apprehending heart*

Expressed in Prim-istent Reality,

it is *Non-striving, Non-resisting* Self of *Pan-gnostic Transexistential Am,*

this *Non-striving, Non-resisting* Self of *Am* Reality (☷),

fused in *universive* Polarity

with *All-embracing Only* Self of *Trans-gnostic Istential Am* (☰)

(pointing respectively to these two third-ring hexagrams in Figure 5).

Second, I Ching's *fifty-third* hexagram.

In Tao of Onliness I Ching it's called

Luminous Recognition Self of *Am*

(pointing to this hexagram in Figure 5):

(*Luminous Recognition* Self of *Am*)

Here is the *image* of this hexagram

(pointing to a photo in his album) (Photo #8),

and these words are its profound Voice of *text*:

> "The individual self,
>
> deluded by forgetfulness
>
> of his identity with the divine Self,
>
> bewildered by his ego,
>
> grieves and is sad.
>
> But when he recognizes the worshipful Lord
>
> as his own Self,
>
> and beholds his glory,

he grieves no more."

- Mundaka

from *The Upanishads*

This, its Tao of Onliness *expression*:

In singular Pan-gnostic Existence;

Am awareness' *boundless Gnostic mind-psyche*

in *fundamental* Polarity with

Am experience's *unconditional Gnostic heart-soul*

Am meaning's *confluent Suffusive mind*

fused in *cardinal* Polarity with

Am communion's *peaceful Infussive heart*

Am inherency's *mind* of *In-ness reflexivity*

in *elemental* Polarity with

Am transparency's *heart* of *Of-ness unreflexivity*

Expressed in Prim-istent Reality,

it is *Luminous Recognition* Self of *Trans-gnostic Transexistential Am*,

this *Luminous Recognition* Self of *Am* Reality ($\equiv\!\equiv$),

fused in *universive* Polarity

with the *No-otherness Trans-istential* Self of *Pan-gnostic Istential Am*

($\equiv\!\equiv$).

(pointing respectively to these two third-ring hexagrams in Figure 5).

Clouds cast shadows on both land and sea.

Recluse watches as these shadows pass.

Drifter muses on his diagram.

Drifter puts his diagram away.

Recluse lies back upon the grass

and looks at blue sky and drifting clouds.

Drifter looks out upon the ocean

rough and choppy in the strong trade winds.

Recluse sits up and turns to drifter.

She picks up a small stone next to her.

Recluse: Learned gypsy,

        conceive this stone to be

        (recluse opens her hand to reveal the stone).

        Here, clutch it, smell it, taste it;

        squeeze it in your hand

        (the vagabond does all of this).

        In Reality, while still itself, it is illusion.

        In this way you are illusion too, and so am I.

        But Self is *neither* illusion *nor* not illusion.

        Beyond sensation, knowledge and conception -

        Self is So!

She points to his hand which holds the stone.

Drifter opens this hand to recluse.

With her finger recluse touches it.

At once the stone explodes in flame.

This whole reality is engulfed

in a tremendous flash of fire;

man, woman, mountain, island, sea, sky -

all of this reality consumed.

The flame alone is and remains.

Slowly it too fades and is no more.

Neither Apparent nor Transparent

nor Parent nor Anti-parent,

unfathomable Being-ness *Is*.

Infinite and All-encompassing.

Both Self-same Seer and That Seen.

Both Realizer and That Realized.

This Is-ness of Unbounded *Form*.

Thusly, only Being-ness "remains."

CHAPTER FOUR

The Flower of Prim-holistent Actlessness

IV

"*Catching the Ox*. Long lost in the wilderness, the boy has at last found the ox and his hands are on him. But, owing to the overwhelming pressure of the outside world, the ox is hard to keep under control. He constantly longs for the old sweet-scented field. The wild nature is still unruly, and altogether refuses to be broken. If the oxherd wishes to see the ox completely in harmony with himself, he has surely to use the whip freely.

> With the energy of his whole being, the boy has at last
> taken hold of the ox:
> But how wild his will, how ungovernable his power!
> At times he struts up a plateau,
> When lo! he is lost again in a misty unpenetrable
> mountain-pass."
> > -from "The Ten Oxherding Pictures"
> > by Kaku-an
> > -compiled by D. T. Suzuki

"This is the Water of Consciousness.

   Drinking from this Wellspring

   We quench Our Thirst of Consciousness.

   Likewise, We are the Water of the Wellspring It Drinks from,

   and Its quenched Thirst of Consciousness."

Learned one stands before the spring

and just behind him stands the mute.

This vagabond hears the mute's strange words,

then leans down and drinks from the small spring.

His thirst is great and he drinks long.

The water tastes very alkaline.

Mute drinks from the spring a long time too.

Learned one, pondering mute's words,

stares vacantly at a distant butte.

For awhile they stand silent there.

Mute looks his same rag-tattered self.

Learned one looks older and tired.

The afternoon air is hot and dry.

In the shade of a cottonwood tree

the two stand at the pipe-fed spring

near the embankment of the river.

Surrounding them are eroded buttes.

The multi-colored layers of rock

of these North Dakota Badlands,

dry and barren in the summer sun.

Desolate and beautiful indeed.

In the shade the two remove their clothes.

Naked, they walk down the embankment

and then into the fast flowing stream.

They float and play and splash about,

they swim and dive and ride the rapids.

Early turns to mid afternoon.

Finally, they walk back to the spring

and once more drink of its cool flow.

The arid breeze dries them as they dress.

Breaking the silence, learned one speaks:

Lo: World-honored One thank you for Your words,

for they awaken a Wellspring in me.

They pack up and walk toward the buttes

through sagebrush and dry prairie grasses.

Through valleys and steep ravines they pass.

On baked gray clay and red "scorio,"

through wild flowers, by green scrub trees,

they walk higher into the Badlands.

Up a steep and rocky butte they climb.

Hot and sweating, they approach the top.

Together, they stand atop its peak.

The strong scent of sage is in the air.

A sea of rugged buttes surround them.

They sit down upon its rounded top

and look out upon this arid land.

They sit in silence and solitude.

Lo: Lost am I in myopic mental maze.

Entangled in unconscious ego life.

Self-contained in world-field folly,

yet glimpsing an Illuminated Path.

Self-enclosed in ego mentality.

Self-entrapped in my own duality.

Attached to my Onliness conception,

obsessed with consensus reality.

World-honored One, I still envy You.

Mute views the distant winding river.

Lost in thought, drifter stares at the ground.

Drifter takes two papers from his pack

and spreads these out on the dry clay.

Lo: This *Tao of Actlessness* Polarity (gesturing to Figure 6).

    Flower of Prim-holistent *Actlessness* (continuing to gesture to Figure 6)

    from Perspective of Tao of Onliness

    as Seen through Pan-gnostic Existent eyes.

    I speak of Tao of Onliness I Ching

    and of Its Actlessness Polarity

    (pointing to the fourth-ring Yin and Yang Actlessness quadrigrams of

    Figure 4).

    These two Prim-holistent *absolute* Realms

    in Prim-ist *absolute* Polarity.

A gust of wind blows across the peak.

Mute looks out upon the rolling buttes.

Drifter continues his monologue.

Lo: These *absolute* Actlessness Realms are called

    Self of *Yang Actlessness* Enlightenment (☱)

    and Self of *Yin Actlessness* Enlightenment (☳),

    here fused in *absolute* Polarity

    (respectively pointing to these two innermost quadrigrams of Figure 6).

    Though Actlessness Ground is Unmanifest,

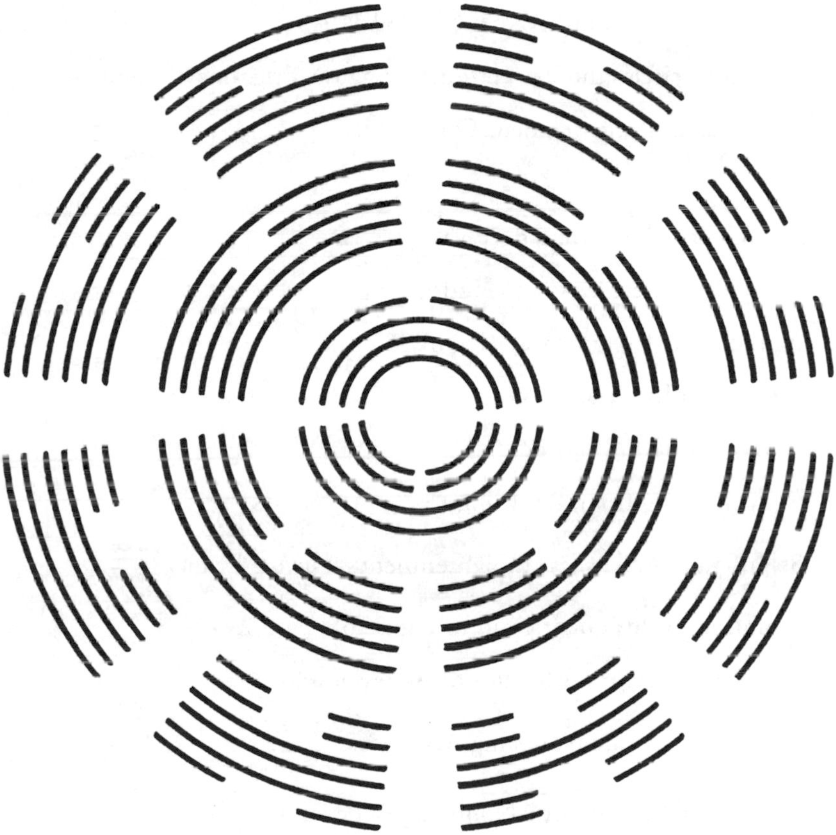

Figure 6

Its Surface Structure *can* be Manifest.

And this is True of *all* Prim-istent Realms.

Each Realm is a Path of Enlightenment

(pointing to the Yin and Yang Actlessness (☷ ☳) Realms in Figure 4)

which Merges with the Other fifteen Paths

(his finger circles the sixteen fourth-ring quadrigrams of Figure 4)

Emerging as Enlightenment Only...

Mute views rocky buttes and deep valleys

shaded here and there as white clouds pass.

Putting the large diagram away (Figure 4),

drifter takes out his photo album.

He returns now to his diagram.

Lo: In turn arising from, returning to

Self of Yang Actlessness Enlightenment's *absolute* Reality (☵)

(pointing to this quadrigram in Figure 6)

are these two *supreme* Realms of Actlessness:

Self of Pan-gnostic Nonbeing Actlessness (☳)

and Self of Trans-gnostic Nonbeing Actlessness (☴)

(pointing respectively to each of these second-ring pentagrams in Figure 6).

Mute stands up, stretches and walks about.

His long hair and beard blow in the breeze.

He looks at the rising crescent moon.

Drifter stands up and joins the mute.

The two watch as a deer grazes

on a slope at the base of the butte.

They return and sit on the butte's peak.

With eyes closed and hands behind his head,

mute lies back upon the bare clay ground.

Learned one turns to his diagram.

Lo: Likewise arising from, returning to

Self of Yin Actlessness Enlightenment's *absolute* Reality (☰)

(pointing to this quadrigram in Figure 6),

the last two *supreme* Realms of Actlessness:

Self of Trans-gnostic Being Actlessness (☴)

in lesser *supreme* Polarity with

Self of Pan-gnostic Nonbeing Actlessness (☳)

(pointing respectively to these two second-ring pentagrams in Figure 6),

and Self of Pan-gnostic Being Actlessness (☱)

in greater *supreme* Polarity with

Self of Trans-gnostic Nonbeing Actlessness (☵)

(pointing respectively to these two second-ring pentagrams in Figure 6).

Learned one glances at the mute

who is fast asleep upon the ground.

He turns and looks out upon the land.

Multi-colored, multi-layered buttes

spreading out as far as eye can see.

Nearby, sagebrush rustles in the wind

and a chipmunk darts from bush to bush.

Drifter views his flower diagram.

Lo: Arising from and thence returning to

supreme Realm's Self of Pan-gnostic Nonbeing Actlessness (☷)

are two *universive* Actlessness Realms:

First, I Ching's *sixty-second* hexagram.

In Tao of Onliness I Ching it's called

Non-discriminating Self of *Actlessness*

(pointing to this hexagram in Figure 6):

(*Non-discriminating* Self of *Actlessness*)

This is the *image* of this hexagram

(pointing to a photo in his album) (Photo #9),

and these words are its profound Voice or *text*:

> "Zen masters give personal guidance in a secluded room.
>
> No one enters while teacher and pupil are together.
>
> Mokurai, the Zen master of Kennin temple in Kyoto,

used to enjoy talking with merchants and newspapermen

as well as his pupils.

A certain tubmaker was almost illiterate.

He would ask foolish questions of Mokurai,

have tea, and then go away.

One day while the tubmaker was there

Mokurai wished to give personal guidance to a disciple,

so he asked the tubmaker to wait in another room.

'I understand you are a living Buddha,' the man protested.

'Even the stone Buddhas in the temple

never refuse the numerous persons who come together before them.

Why then should I be excluded?'

Mokurai had to go outside to see his disciple."

-from *Zen Flesh, Zen Bones*

compiled by Paul Reps

This, its Tao of Onliness *expression:*

In singular Pan-gnostic Existence;

Actless awareness' *Form* of *nonduality*

Actless meaning's *mind* of *Eternity*

Actless inherency's *mind* of *Deep Repose*

Expressed in Prim-istent Reality,

it is *Non-discriminating* Self of *Pan-gnostic Istential Actlessness.*

This *Non-discriminating* Self of Actlessness Reality (☷)

(pointing to this third-ring hexagram in Figure 6).

Second, I Ching's *fifty-sixth* hexagram.

In Tao of Onliness I Ching it's called

Changeless Self of *Actlessness*

(pointing to this hexagram in Figure 6):

(*Changeless* Self of *Actlessness*)

Here is the *image* of this hexagram

(pointing to a photo in his album) (Photo #10),

and these words are its profound Voice or *text*:

"Those who know don't talk.
Those who talk don't know.

Close your mouth, block off your senses,
blunt your sharpness, untie your knots,
soften your glare, settle your dust.
This is primal identity.

Be like the Tao.
It can't be approached or withdrawn from,
benefited or harmed, honored or brought into disgrace.
It gives itself up continually.

That is why it endures.

- Lao-tzu from *Tao Te Ching*

Stephen Mitchell Translation

This, its Tao of Onliness *expression*:

In singular Pan-gnostic Existence;

Actless awareness' *vision* of *holo-ceptive Unconditionality*

Actless meaning's trans-symbolic *Prehending mind*

Actless inherency's *scient mind* of *Reflection*

Expressed in Prim-istent Reality,

it is *Changeless* Self of *Trans gnostic Istential Actlessness*.

This *Changeless* Self of Actlessness Reality (☰)

(pointing to this third-ring hexagram in Figure 6).

Gusting winds blow in late afternoon.

Billowing white clouds float high above.

Mute remains asleep upon the ground.

Drifter weights his paper with a stone

to keep it from sailing in the wind.

Drifter stands and walks about the peak

looking out across this wilderness.

Among this sea of rolling buttes

the Little Missouri River winds.

Mute opens his eyes and sits up.

Drifter returns and sits next to mute.

Arising, the two walk off the peak

down to a rock-ledge outcropping

whereon they seat themselves full-lotus.

Facing the rock wall, they sit zazen.

Thusly they meditate an hour.

After this, they return to the peak

and seat themselves facing the River.

Mute sits erect with his eyes closed.

Vagabond looks down at his paper.

Lo: Freely arising from, returning to

   supreme Realm's Self of Trans-gnostic Being Actlessness (☰)

   are two *universive* Actlessness Realms:

   First, this *ninth* hexagram of the I Ching.

   In Tao of Onliness I Ching it's called

   God-realized Self of *Actlessness*

   (pointing to this hexagram in Figure 6):

(*God-realized* Self of *Actlessness*)

Here is the *image* of this hexagram

(pointing to a photo in his album) (Photo #11),

and these words are its profound Voice or *text*:

"My teachings are easy to understand

and easy to put into practice.

Yet your intellect will never grasp them,

and if you try to practice them, you'll fail.

My teachings are older than the world.

How can you grasp their meaning?

If you want to know me,

look inside your heart."

- Lao-tzu from *Tao Te Ching*

Stephen Mitchell Translation

This, its Tao of Onliness *expression*:

In singular Pan-gnostic Existence;

Actless experience's *Void* of *eternity*

in *fundamental* Polarity with

Actless awareness' *Form* of *nonduality*

Actless communion's *heart* of *Nonduality*

fused in *cardinal* Polarity with

Actless meaning's *mind* of *Eternity*

Actless transparency's *heart* of *Homeward Voyager*

in *elemental* Polarity with

Actless inherency's *mind* of *Deep Repose*

Expressed in Prim-istent Reality,

it is *God-realized* Self of *Trans-gnostic Transexistential Actlessness*,

this *God-realized* Self of Actlessness Reality (☷),

fused in *universive* Polarity

with *Non-discriminating* Self of *Pan-gnostic Istential Actlessness* (☵)

(pointing respectively to these two third-ring hexagrams in Figure 6).

Second, this *fifth* hexagram of I Ching.

In Tao of Onliness I Ching it's called

No-thingness, No-mind Self of *Actlessness*

(pointing to this hexagram in Figure 6):

(*No-thingness, No-mind* Self of *Actlessness*)

Here is the *image* of this hexagram

(pointing to a photo in his album) (Photo #12),

and these words are its profound Voice or *text*:

> "The Tao that can be told is not the eternal Tao.
> The name that can be named is not the eternal Name.

The unnameable is the eternally real.

Naming is the origin of all particular things.

Free from desire, you realize the mystery.

Caught in desire, you see only the manifestations.

Yet mystery and manifestations arise from the same source.

This source is called darkness.

Darkness within darkness.

The gateway to all understanding."

- Lao-tzu from *Tao Te Ching*

Stephen Mitchell Translation

This, its Tao of Onliness *expression*:

In singular Pan-gnostic Existence;

Actless experience's *power* of *trans-ceptive Boundlessness*

in *fundamental* Polarity with

Actless awareness' *vision* of *holo-ceptive Unconditionality*

Actless communion's trans-symbolic *Conceptive heart*

fused in *cardinal* Polarity with

Actless meaning's trans-symbolic *Prehending mind*

Actless transparency's *lucent heart* of *Bliss*

in *elemental* Polarity with

Actless inherency's *scient mind* of *Reflection*

Expressed in Prim-istent Reality,

it is *No-thingness, No-mind* Self of *Pan-gnostic Transexistential Actlessness*,

this *No-thingness, No-mind* Self of Actlessness Reality (☷),

fused in *universive* Polarity

with *Changeless* Self of *Trans-gnostic Istential Actlessness* (☶)

(pointing respectively to these two third-ring hexagrams in Figure 6).

On cue, mute's flatulence resounds.

Learned one smiles and shakes his head.

Mute is looking down at the cracked clay

covering the top of this bare butte.

Drifter gets up, stretches and yawns

while from the backpack mute removes

a jar of water, two bananas,

thermos of soup with an attached cup,

peanuts, and tuna sandwiches.

They share this supper in silence.

After eating, they put things away.

Thunder clouds are building to the West.

An eagle circles high above them.

Mute lies down upon the warm dry clay

and watches the eagle in its flight.

Drifter looks down at his diagram.

Lo: Arising from and thence returning to

supreme Realm's Self of Trans-gnostic Nonbeing Actlessness (☳)

are two *universive* Actlessness Realms:

First, this *thirty-first* I Ching hexagram.

In Tao of Onliness I Ching it's called

Trans-egoic Meritless Self of *Actlessness*

(pointing to this hexagram in Figure 6):

(*Trans-egoic Meritless* Self of *Actlessness*)

Here is the *image* of this hexagram

(pointing to a photo in his album) (Photo #13),

and these words are its profound Voice or *text*:

"Yamaoka Tesshu, as a young student of Zen,

visited one master after another.

He called upon Dokuon of Shokoku.

Desiring to show his attainment, he said:

'The mind, Buddha, and sentient beings, after all, do not exist.

The true nature of phenomena is emptiness.

There is no realization, no delusion, no sage, no mediocrity.

There is no giving and nothing to be received.'

Dokuon, who was smoking quietly, said nothing.

Suddenly he whacked Yamaoka with his bamboo pipe.

This made the youth quite angry.

'If nothing exists,' inquired Dokuon,

'where did this anger come from?' "

- from *Zen Flesh, Zen Bones*

compiled by Paul Reps

This, its Tao of Onliness *expression*:

In singular Pan-gnostic Existence;

Actless awareness' *omniscient* Consciousness

Actless meaning's *boundless Convergent mind*

Actless inherency's *mind*: *hidden wellspring* of Worlds

Expressed in Prim-istent Reality,

it is *Trans-egoic Meritless* Self of *Pan-gnostic Antistential Actlessness*.

This *Trans-egoic Meritless* Self of Actlessness Reality (☶)

(pointing to this third-ring hexagram in Figure 6).

Second, I Ching's *thirty-third* hexagram.

In Tao of Onliness I Ching it's called

Inherent, Illuminated Self of *Actlessness*

(pointing to this hexagram in Figure 6):

(*Inherent, Illuminated* Self of *Actlessness*)

Here is the *image* of this hexagram
(pointing to a photo in his album) (Photo #14),
and these words are its profound Voice or *text*:

"I Am The Servant and The Realizer Of The Divine Person,

The Self-Radiant and Self-Existing Being,

The Person or Condition That Is Even Your Own Consciousness

(Prior To the body-mind and the self-Contraction).

Here I AM, Always Alive With You,

Calling To The Divine Self (Who Is You, The Very Self).

'I AM' Is The Way That I Teach.

The Way Is To Recognize and To Realize

The Divine Person As Your Real or Original Self,

Through The Ordeal Of Transcendence Of the conditional self."

- Da Free John

from *The Dawn Horse Testament*

This, its Tao of Onliness *expression*:

In singular Pan-gnostic Existence;

Actless awareness' trans-mental *mind-psyche* of *Reflexivity*

Actless meaning's *Trans-scient mind*

Actless inherency's *mind* of *meaning's Void*

Expressed in Prim-istent Reality,

it is *Inherent, Illuminated* Self of *Trans-gnostic Antistential Actlessness.*

This *Inherent, Illuminated* Self of Actlessness Reality (☴)

(pointing to this third-ring hexagram in Figure 6).

Mute and drifter sitting on the butte
cast long shadows across its domed top.
Drifter gazes out on the Badlands.
Crimson shadows fill its deep valleys.

The two stand and walk down from the peak
and into a canyon far below.
Mute and drifter stop to urinate.
They walk on toward the valley floor
among sage, dry grass and tumbleweed.

The sinking sun casts an amber glow
coloring this rocky wilderness.
As they pass, a rabbit stands stark still.
Birds fly from tree to tree about them
filling the evening air with song.

The two stop and sit upon a rock
at the mouth of a deep ravine.
Mute fills, lights up and smokes his pipe.

A rattlesnake suddenly appears

gliding out from underneath the rock.

It stops directly before drifter

and starts to rattle furiously.

Gasping, drifter scrambles up the rock.

Ten feet away, mute sits very still.

Drifter stares intently at the snake

rattling on the ground below.

In this moment drifter's mind is clear;

free of egoic mind wandering.

Fixed and focused on this potent snake.

Fearful of egoic self-sense death,

holding fast to his egoic life.

Suddenly he Sees this clingingness,

and Knows this illusion he clings to.

The rattlesnake soon glides away

through the sage toward the deep ravine.

Motionless, they sit upon the rock.

Drifter calmly sits there for a time

and resumes his normal consciousness.

The two climb down and walk to the butte.

Reaching it, they climb to the top.

Here they sit together at the peak.

Mute looks out upon this rugged land

glowing in the evening's setting sun.

Drifter takes out his diagram

and spreads it before them on the ground.

Lo: Likewise arising from, returning to

supreme Realm's Self of Pan-gnostic Being Actlessness (☷)

are two *universive* Actlessness Realms:

First, this *twenty-sixth* I Ching hexagram.

In Tao of Onliness it's called

Unconditional Self of *Actlessness*

(pointing to this hexagram in Figure 6):

(*Unconditional* Self of *Actlessness*)

Here is the *image* of this hexagram

(pointing to a photo in his album) (Photo #15),

and these words are its profound Voice or *text*:

"Just before Ninakawa passed away the Zen master Ikkyu visited him.

'Shall I lead you on?' Ikkyu asked.

Ninakawa replied: 'I came here alone and I go alone.

What help could you be to me?'

Ikkyu answered: 'If you think you really come and go,

that is your delusion.

Let me show you the path

on which there is no coming and no going.'

With his words, Ikkyu had revealed the path so clearly

that Ninakawa smiled and passed away."

- from *Zen Flesh, Zen Bones*

compiled by Paul Reps

This, its Tao of Onliness *expression*:

In singular Pan-gnostic Existence;

Actless experience's *omnipotent* Consciousness

in *fundamental* Polarity with

Actless awareness' *omniscient* Consciousness

Actless communion's *unconditional Vergent heart*

fused in *cardinal* Polarity with

Actless meaning's *boundless Convergent mind*

Actless transparency's *heart: perfect emptiness* of Worlds

in *elemental* Polarity with

Actless inherency's *mind: hidden wellspring* of Worlds

Expressed in Prim-istent Reality,

it is *Unconditional* Self of *Trans-gnostic Existential Actlessness*,

this *Unconditional* Self of Actlessness Reality (☲),

fused in *universive* Polarity

with *Trans-egoic Meritless* Self of *Pan-gnostic Antistential Actlessness* (☰)

(pointing respectively to these two third-ring hexagrams in Figure 6).

Second, I Ching's *eleventh* hexagram.

In Tao of Onliness I Ching it's called

Unutterable Transcendental Self of *Actlessness*

(pointing to this hexagram in Figure 6):

(*Unutterable Transcendental* Self of *Actlessness*)

Here is the *image* of this hexagram

(pointing to a photo in his album) (Photo #16),

and these words are its profound Voice or *text*:

> "I tell you solemnly, before Abraham ever was, I Am."
>
> - Jesus
>
> from *The Jerusalem Bible*

This, its Tao of Onliness *expression*:

In singular Pan-gnostic Existence;

Actless experience's trans-mental *heart-soul* of *Unreflexivity*

in *fundamental* Polarity with

Actless awareness' trans-mental *mind-psyche* of *Reflextivity*

Actless communion's *Holo-lucent heart*

fused in *cardinal* Polarity with

Actless meaning's *Trans-scient mind*

Actless transparency's *heart* of *communion's Void*

in *elemental* Polarity with

Actless inherency's *mind* of *meaning's Void*

Expressed in Prim-istent Reality,

it is *Unutterable Transcendental* Self of *Pan-gnostic Existential Actlessness,*

this *Unutterable Transcendental* Self of Actlessness Reality (☱),

fused in *universive* Polarity

with *Inherent, Illuminated* Self of *Trans-gnostic Antistential Actlessness*

(☴)

(pointing respectively to these two third-ring hexagrams in Figure 6).

Twilight illuminates the Badlands.

Strong gusts of wind blow upon the butte.

Mute cleans his pipe and puts it away.

A long silence rests between the two.

Black thunder clouds now fill the sky.

Booming thunder fills the air with sound.

Dark veils of rain fall to the West.

Learned one looks into the mute's face

whose peaceful eyes stare in deep repose.

Mute points to a tree near the butte's top.

A bright lightning flash cuts through the air

and with it deafening thunder.

At once, the tree ignites in flame.

The fire grows in ferocity.

Suddenly this fire conflagrates,

exploding like a firestorm.

Engulfing *all* that is in view;

mute, drifter, butte, river, Badlands, sky -

it consumes this *whole* reality.

The fire alone is and remains.

Slowly it too fades and is no more.

Neither Apparent nor Transparent

nor Parent nor Anti-parent,

fathomless Nonbeing-ness *Is-not*.

Both Anti-seer and Anti-seen.

Anti-Realizer-Realized.

This Is-not-ness of Unbounded *Void*.

Thus, only Nonbeing-ness "remains."

CHAPTER FIVE

The Flower of Prim-holistent Radiance

V

"*Herding the Ox*. When a thought moves, another follows, and then another—an endless train of thoughts is thus awakened. Through enlightenment all this turns into truth; but falsehood asserts itself when confusion prevails. Things oppress us not because of an objective world, but because of a self-deceiving mind. Do not let the nose-string loose, hold it tight, and allow no vacillation.

> The boy is not to separate himself with his whip and
>   tether,
> Lest the animal should wander away into a world of
>   defilements;
> When the ox is properly tended to, he will grow pure
>   and docile;
> Without a chain, nothing binding, he will by himself
>   follow the oxherd."

-from "The Ten Oxherding Pictures"
by Kaku-an
-compiled by D. T. Suzuki
from *Manual of Zen Buddhism*

At crest and precipice of seacliff
with the half-moon high above them
learned man and recluse woman stand.
Far below the waves are crashing
and the ocean spreads before them.
Long they stand like this together
looking out on the blue ocean.

They walk from the seacliff summit.
Down the sloping cliff they wander
on the rocky ledges walking
over zig-zag paths together
toward their place of meditation.
Climbing up a rocky side-path
to a ledge of rock and grasses,
here they sit facing the twilit sea.
Dwarfed and isolated figures
on this ledge of towering seacliff

overlooking these vast waters.

For a long time they sit silent

and then the recluse woman speaks:

Recluse: The Wind of Illumination

blows everywhere and nowhere *all* the same.

Vagabond, See Me *beyond* shadows.

Know Me as the *Truth* I Am.

I Am Illumination's Wind.

Hear My silent Words.

Birthless, Deathless, Boundless, and Unconditional,

I Am *Reality*.

They sit silent looking out to sea.

Lo: It's true, I know You only as shadow;

see You only through these egoic eyes.

I cling to my conditionality.

I clutch this world-field manifold

of mind illusion and conditioning

as if it were the only thing I trust.

It is egoic self-sense I embrace.

It is to this ego-world I cling.

Trying to outmaneuver this bound self

which is far beyond my capacity.

Mired in sensation and desire

and chasing my own egoic tail.

Sage, nonetheless I thank You for Your words.

They Illuminate this dark path for me.

They sit in silence facing Northward

looking out upon the water

as darkness overcomes the twilight.

Taking two papers from his backpack

learned one spreads these before them,

their patterns visible by moonlight.

Lo: This *Tao of Radiance* Polarity (gesturing to Figure 7).

  Flower of Prim-holistent Radiance (continuing to gesture to Figure 7)

  from Perspective of Tao of Onliness

  as Seen through Pan-gnostic Existent eyes.

  I speak of Tao of Onliness I Ching

  and of Its *Radiance* Polarity

  (pointing to the fourth-ring Yin and Yang Radiance quadrigrams of

  Figure 4).

  These *absolute* Radiance Realms are called

  Self of *Yang Radiance* Enlightenment ($\equiv\equiv$)

  and *Self* of *Yin Radiance* Enlightenment ($\equiv\ \equiv$),

  here fused in *absolute* Polarity

  (pointing respectively to these two innermost quadrigrams of Figure 7).

Two Enlightenment Paths of Radiance

(pointing to the Yin and Yang Radiance (☱☲   ☷) Realms in Figures 4 and 7).

Reaching for the drifter's backpack,

recluse woman pulls it to her.

She takes scrap wood and paper from it.

Some of this she piles before them,

strikes a match and lights a fire.

Its amber glow lights up the darkness.

The flame begins to crack and spark.

Scent of burning wood soon fills the air.

Recluse stands up and walks about,

stopping to look down at breaking surf.

Meanwhile the ragged vagabond

wraps one potato then another

tightly in some metal foil

also taken from his backpack.

These he drops into the fire.

The wind gusts and sparks fly in his face.

He wildly fans them with his hands,

then quickly rolls away from the flame

and briefly lies flat upon the ground.

Returning, recluse stands above him.

She smiles broadly, then they both laugh.

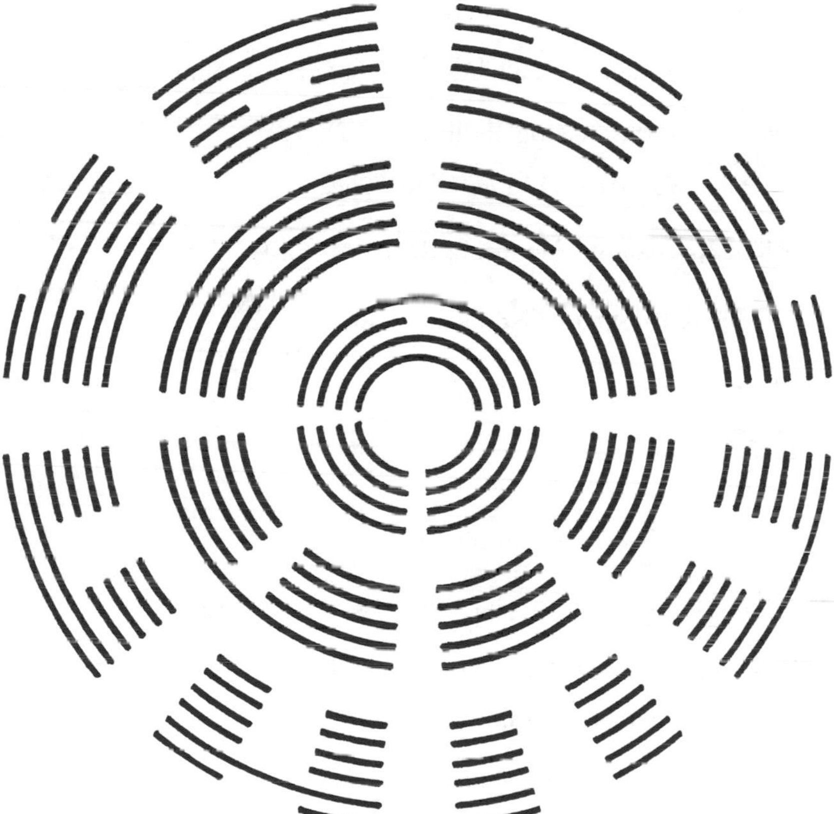

Figure 7

Soon both of them sit before the flame.

Putting the large diagram away (Figure 4),

drifter takes out his photo album.

He turns to his flower diagram (Figure 7).

Lo: Freely arising from, returning to

Self of Yang Radiance Enlightenment's *absolute* Reality (☰)

(pointing to this quadrigram in Figure 7)

are these two *supreme* Realms of Radiance:

Self of Trans-gnostic Nonbeing Radiance (☳)

and Self of Pan-gnostic Nonbeing Radiance (☳)

(pointing respectively to each of these two second-ring pentagrams in Figure 7).

Likewise arising from, returning to

Self of Yin Radiance Enlightenment's *absolute* Reality (☷)

(pointing to this quadrigram in Figure 7)

are two more *supreme* Realms of Radiance:

Self of Pan-gnostic Being Radiance (☶)

in greater *supreme* Polarity with

Self of Trans-gnostic Nonbeing Radiance (☳)

(pointing respectively to these two second-ring pentagrams in Figure 7),

and Self of Trans-gnostic Being Radiance (☵)

in lesser *supreme* Polarity with

Self of Pan-gnostic Nonbeing Radiance (☰)

(pointing respectively to these two second-ring pentagrams in Figure 7).

Two figures sit before the fire
looking out upon this windblown sea.

Recluse lies down on grass and earth.
Yawning, she stretches on the ground.
Drifter leans back upon a rock,
closes his eyes and soon falls asleep.
The fire burns, stars fill the sky,
tropic moonlight shimmers on the sea.

The cry of a gull awakens him.
In vain, his eyes search to see the gull,
then he looks at recluse lying there.
She looks back and makes a sharp gull cry.
He shakes his head and smiles, then laughs.
Soon both lie in laughter on the ground.
After a time they are silent there,
gazing upward at a sky of stars.

Learned one adds wood to the fire.
He unfolds his paper on the ground.
Lo: Again arising from, returning to

supreme Realm's Self of Trans-gnostic Nonbeing Radiance (☷)

are two *universive* Radiance Realms:

First, this *tenth* hexagram of the I Ching.

In Tao of Onliness I Ching it's called

All-inclusive Self of *Radiance*

(pointing to this hexagram in Figure 7):

(*All-inclusive* Self of *Radiance*)

Here is the *image* of this hexagram

(pointing to a photo in his album) (Photo #17),

and Mute's words are its profound Voice or *text*:

> "This stone (mute holds in his hand)
>
> is the Self-same Consciousness I Am."
>
> - Mute Sage

This, its Tao of Onliness *expression*:

In singular Pan-gnostic Existence;

Radiance experience's *genesis* of *Creativity*

Radiance communion's *Seeing heart*

Radiance serenity's *heart* of *one all-where Singularity*

Expressed in Prim-istent Reality,

it is *All-inclusive* Self of *Trans-gnostic Antistential Radiance.*

This *All-inclusive* Self of Radiance Reality (☷)

(pointing to this third-ring hexagram in Figure 7).

Second, I Ching's *fifty-eighth* hexagram.

In Tao of Onliness I Ching it's called

Compassionate Omniscient Self of *Radiance*

(pointing to this hexagram in Figure 7):

(*Compassionate Omniscient* Self of *Radiance*)

Here is the *image* of this hexagram

(pointing to a photo in his album) (Photo #18),

and these words are its profound Voice or *text*:

> "A monk told Joshu: 'I have just entered the the monastery.
> Please teach me.'
> Joshu asked: 'Have you eaten your rice porridge?'
> The monk replied: 'I have eaten.'
> Joshu said: 'Then you had better wash your bowl.'
> At that moment the monk was enlightened.

Mumon's comment: Joshu is the man who opens his mouth
and shows his heart.

I doubt if this monk really saw Joshu's heart.

I hope he did not mistake the bell for the pitcher.

It is too clear and so it is hard to see.

A dunce once searched for fire with a lighted lantern.

Had he known what fire was,

He could have cooked his rice much sooner."

- from *Zen Flesh, Zen Bones*

compiled by Paul Reps

This, its Tao of Onliness *expression*:

In singular Pan-gnostic Existence;

Radiance experience's trans-symbolic *transfigurative* Self

Radiance communion's *Omnipotent heart*

Radiance serenity's *heart*: *foundation* and *awakening* of Worlds

Expressed in Prim-istent Reality,

it is *Compassionate Omniscient* Self of *Pan-gnostic Antistential Radiance*.

This *Compassionate Omniscient* Self of Radiance Reality (☶)

(pointing to this third-ring hexagram in Figure 7).

The fire begins to die away.

Drifter puts more wood upon the flame,

shifting his potatoes with a stick.

Drifter gazes at the burning flame.

Recluse is asleep upon the ground.

Soon she awakens and sits upright.

She too looks into the dancing flame.

Recluse picks up learned one's paper,

suspending it above the fire.

Learned one is startled and surprised.

Quickly he grasps his diagram,

saving it from the consuming flame.

Recluse woman is most amused.

She gets up and dances round the flame.

Vagabond watches her and laughs.

Soon he joins her, dancing round about.

Finally they both fall to the ground,

lying silent there among the stars.

After a time learned one sits up

and puts his diagram before him.

Lo: Likewise arising from, returning to

supreme Realm's Self of Pan-gnostic Being Radiance (☷)

are two universive Radiance Realms:

First, this second hexagram of I Ching.

In Tao of Onliness I Ching it's called

Eternal Self of *Radiance*

(pointing to this hexagram in Figure 7):

(*Eternal* Self of *Radiance*)

Here is the *image* of this hexagram

(pointing to a photo in his album) (Photo #19),

and these words its initial Voice or *text*:

"Chuang-tzu was fishing one time in the P'u River.

Two ministers came up. They said they were ministers from the King of

Ch'u.

The King of Ch'u wanted Chuang-tzu to come and run his kingdom for

him.

Chuang-tzu sat there and held his fishing pole.

He didn't even turn around. And he said to the ministers,

'Doesn't your king have a sacred tortoise

that's been dead for three thousand years,

and doesn't the king keep his tortoise wrapped up and in a box

and stored in his ancestral temple?'

'Yes, that's no lie,' said the ministers.

And Chuang-tzu said, 'This tortoise, is he better off dead

and with his boned venerated, or is he better off alive

with his tail dragging in his mud?'

And the ministers said, 'Better off alive, we suppose,

with his tail dragging in the mud.'

'Go away,' said Chuang-tzu, 'and let me drag my tail in the mud.' "

- from *The Taoist Vision*

Translated by William

McNaughton

and these words, its completed Voice or *text*:

"If you push forward with your last ounce of strength

at the very point where the path of your thinking has been blocked,

and then, completely stymied,

leap with hands high in the air

into the tremendous abyss of fire confronting you -

into the ever-burning flame of your own primordial nature -

all ego-consciousness, all delusive feelings and thoughts and perceptions

will perish with your ego-root

and the true source of your Self-nature will appear."

- Bassui's letter to Layman Ippo

from *The Three Pillars of Zen*

by Roshi Philip Kapleau (Editor)

This, its Tao of Onliness *expression*:

In singular Pan-gnostic Existence;

Radiance awareness' *morphosis* of *Productivity*

in *fundamental* Polarity with

Radiance experience's *genesis* of *Creativity*

Radiance meaning's *Envisioning mind*

fused in *cardinal* Polarity with

Radiance communion's *Seeing heart*

Radiance multiplicity's *mind* of *none each-where Radiance*

in *elemental* Polarity with

Radiance serenity's *heart* of *one all-where Singularity*

Expressed in Prim-istent Reality,

it is *Eternal* Self of *Pan-gnostic Existential Radiance*,

this *Eternal* Self of Radiance Reality (☷),

fused in *universive* Polarity

with *All-inclusive* Self of *Trans-gnostic Antistential Radiance* (☳)

(pointing respectively to these two third-ring hexagrams in Figure 7).

Second, I Ching's *twenty-third* hexagram.

In Tao of Onliness I Ching it's called

Choiceless Self of *Radiance*

(pointing to this hexagram in Figure 7):

(*Choiceless* Self of *Radiance*)

Here is the *image* of this hexagram

(pointing to a photo in his album) (Photo #20),

and these words are its profound Voice or *text*:

"A Zen master named Gisan asked a young student

to bring him a pail of water to cool his bath.

The student brought the water and, after cooling the bath,

threw on to the ground the little that was left over.

'You dunce!' the master scolded him.

'Why didn't you give the rest of the water to the plants?

What right have you to waste even a drop of water in this temple?'

The young student attained Zen in that instant.

He changed his name to Tekisui,

which means a drop of water."

- from *Zen Flesh, Zen Bones*

compiled by Paul Reps

This, its Tao of Onliness *expression*:

In singular Pan-gnostic Existence;

Radiance awareness' trans-symbolic *configurative* Self

in *fundamental* Polarity with

Radiance experience's trans-symbolic *transfigurative* Self

Radiance meaning's *Omniscient mind*

fused in *cardinal* Polarity with

Radiance communion's *Omnipotent heart*

Radiance multiplicity's mind: *consumation* and *illumination* of Worlds

in *elemental* Polarity with

Radiance serenity's heart: *foundation* and *awakening* of Worlds

Expressed in Prim-istent Reality,

it is *Choiceless* Self of *Trans-gnostic Existential Radiance*,

this *Choiceless* Self of Radiance Reality (☰☰),

fused in *universive* Polarity

with *Compassionate Omniscient* Self of *Pan-gnostic Antistential Radiance*

(☷)

(pointing respectively to these two third-ring hexagrams in Figure 7).

Learned on looks out upon the sea.

Glowing embers cast dim firelight.

The small flame flickers in the darkness.

Recluse woman sits with her eyes closed.

Scent of blooming Jasmine fills the air.

Drifter, with a stick maneuver,

moves the two potatoes from the flame.

With spoons, spread, and pepper from the pack,

they season and eat their potatoes,

and from a jar they drink apple juice.

After clean-up of their midnight snack,

recluse gets up and walks about.

She looks at the moon, then out to sea.

Drifter puts more wood upon the flame.

Recluse stands at the ledge precipice

listening to gulls and pounding surf.

Drifter watches as the fire grows.

Drifter now spreads out his diagram.

Lo: Once more, arising from, returning to

supreme Realm's Self of Pan-gnostic Nonbeing Radiance (☲)

are two universive Radiance Realms:

First, this thirty-eighth I Ching hexagram

In Tao of Onliness I Ching it's called

Brahman-consciousness (Atman) Self of Radiance

(pointing to this hexagram in Figure 7):

(Brahman-consciousness (Atman) Self of Radiance)

Here is the image of this hexagram

(pointing to a photo in his album) (Photo #21),

and Your words are its profound Voice or text:

"Learned vagabond, you stumble on in darkness

of mental attribution shadows.

Asleep in thought illusion,

stranded in vacant worlds.

Beloved, what emptiness your Heart must long endure."

- Recluse Sage

This, its Tao of Onliness *expression*:

In singular Pan-gnostic Existence;

Radiance experience's *power* of *trans-ceptive Boundlessness*

Radiance communion's *heart* of *one all-where* Consciousness

Radiance serenity's *lucent heart* of *Potency*

Expressed in Prim-istent Reality,

it is *Brahman-consciousness (Atman)* Self of *Trans-gnostic Istential Radiance.*

This *Brahman-consciousness (Atman)* Self of Radiance Reality (☰)

(pointing to this third-ring hexagram in Figure 7).

Second, I Ching's *fifty-fourth* hexagram.

In Tao of Onliness I Ching it's called

Suchness Self of *Radiance*

(pointing to this hexagram in Figure 7):

(*Suchness* Self of *Radiance*)

Here is the *image* of this hexagram

(pointing to a photo in his album) (Photo #22),

and Mute's words are its profound Voice or *text*:

"Listen to the wind among the pines

(pointing to the pine trees above them).

It whispers one Word only - 'Consciousness'.

Fish-catcher of visionary dreams,

I Am *Self* - boundless, birthless, deathless.

No-thing at All.

I Am Enlightenment *with no second.*

Fish-fryer of luminous schemes,

I Am.

Beloved, You and I are *One* Destiny!

We *are* Consciousness, Wind among the Pines!"

- Mute Sage

This, its Tao of Onliness *expression*:

In singular Pan-gnostic Existence;

Radiance experience's *Void* of *eternity*

Radiance communion's *Transfigurative heart*

Radiance serenity's *Contemplative heart*

Expressed in Prim-istent Reality,

it is *Suchness* Self of *Pan-gnostic Istential Radiance.*

This *Suchness* Self of Radiance Reality (☵)

(pointing to this third-ring hexagram in Figure 7).

Turning, drifter looks at the recluse

whose face glows in the firelight.

Recluse looks upon the moonlit sea.

Surf pounds on the rocky cliffs below.

Lo: Sage, You, this fire, these gulls, this seacliff,

this moon, these stars, and this majestic sea -

I Am all This, This is I Am.

We are One and the Same Self-radiance.

Beyond this manifest subject-object duality

of my embodied conditional and bounded consciousness,

I Am *Self*, timeless, boundless, unconditional.

Recluse turns and looks into his face.

Drifter views shimmering moonlit sea.

Recluse lies back and looks at the moon.

The fire burns down to a small flame.

Recluse stands up, yawns and stretches.

Drifter gets up and walks about,

finally stopping before the flame.

They stand face to face across the flame.

Recluse views the burning embers' glow

while drifter intently views her face.

Soon she sits down and drifter joins her.

In silence, they view the dying flame.

Drifter spreads his paper on the ground.

Lo: Freely arising from, returning to

supreme Realm's Self of Trans-gnostic Being Radiance (☰ ☰)

are two universive Radiance Realms:

First, this eighth hexagram of the I Ching.

In Tao of Onliness I Ching it's called

Christ-consciousness Self of Radiance

(pointing to this hexagram in Figure 7):

☵

(Christ-consciousness Self of Radiance)

Here is the image of this hexagram

(pointing to a photo in his album) (Photo #23),

and Your words are its profound Voice or text:

> "Child of Consciousness,
> know that every thing returns
> complete unto Itself.
> Unto the Oneness of Its infinity.
> Unto the Self-realizing mirror
> of Its Awakening.

Unto Its own transparent self-abiding Am."

- Recluse Sage

from *The Tao of Onliness: An I Ching*
Cosmology - The Awakening Years

This, its Tao of Onliness *expression*:

In singular Pan-gnostic Existence;

Radiance awareness' *vision* of *holo-ceptive Unconditionality*

in *fundamental* Polarity with

Radiance experience's *power* of *trans-ceptive Boundlessness*

Radiance meaning's *mind* of *none each-where* Consciousness

fused in *cardinal* Polarity with

Radiance communion's *heart* of *one all-where* Consciousness

Radiance multiplicity's *scient mind* of *Vision*

in *elemental* Polarity with

Radiance serenity's *lucent heart* of *Potency*

Expressed in Prim-istent Reality,

it is *Christ-consciousness* Self of *Pan-gnostic Transexistential Radiance*,

this *Christ-consiousness* Self of Radiance Reality (☷),

fused in *universive* Polarity

with *Brahman-consciousness (Atman)* Self of *Trans-gnostic Istential*

Radiance (☶)

(pointing respectively to these two third-ring hexagrams in Figure 7).

Second, I Ching's *twentieth* hexagram.

In Tao of Onliness I Ching it's called

Seamless Self of *Radiance*

(pointing to this hexagram in Figure 7):

(*Seamless* Self of *Radiance*)

Here is the *image* of this hexagram
(pointing to a photo in his album) (Photo #24),
and Your words are its profound Voice or *text*:

> "Island, sea, and crystal dreams,
>
> which is the seer and which the seen?
>
> Flickering light of shadow streams,
>
> which is the seemer and which the seemed?
>
>
> Eye of Onliness vagabond,
>
> I Am *beyond* duality, *beyond* boundary, *beyond* conditionality.
>
> I Am Enlightenment *with no second*.
>
> Visionary word carpenter,
>
> *I Am*.
>
> Beloved, You and I are *One* Destiny!
>
> We are seamless Eternity!"
>
> - Recluse Sage

This, its Tao of Onliness *expression*:

In singular Pan-gnostic Existence;

Radiance awareness' *Form* of *nonduality*

in *fundamental* Polarity with

Radiance experience's *Void* of *eternity*

Radiance meaning's *Configurative mind*

fused in *cardinal* Polarity with

Radiance communion's *Transfigurative heart*

Radiance multiplicity's *Illuminative mind*

in *elemental* Polarity with

Radiance serenity's *Contemplative heart*

Expressed in Prim-istent Reality,

it is *Seamless* Self of *Trans-gnostic Transexistential Radiance*,

this *Seamless* Self of Radiance Reality (☲),

fused in *universive* Polarity

with *Suchness* Self of *Pan-gnostic Istential Radiance* (☶)

(pointing respectively to these two third-ring hexagrams in Figure 7).

Learned one looks up and out to sea.

Moonlit clouds rest on the horizon.

He hears breakers crashing on the rocks

and inhales the scent of salt sea air.

Recluse lies asleep upon the ground.

Recluse wakens, and slowly sits up.

She turns to view the setting moon,

then turns to look at the learned one.

Recluse: Weaver of conception,

embrace your own self-sense mortality.

Know it indifferently

as neither real nor unreal, and both.

Realize *Self* only.

Not just in your mind, but in your Heart.

Choicelessly, Be Noneother Than.

The vagabond sits in silence.

Recluse woman walks to the cliff ledge,

strikes a match and throws it to the wind.

At once the air ignites in flame,

exploding in a burst of fire

which engulfs the *whole* atmosphere.

Man, woman, cliff, island, sea and sky -

all of this reality consumed.

The flame alone is and remains.

Slowly it too fades and is no more.

Beyond *both* Being and Nonbeing,

all-inclusive Self that's *only* Self,

this Self of Onliness Manifests -

Yin and Yang Onliness *Prim-holist*.

Unfathomable, unknowable,

thus *This* Prim-holisting-ness "remains."

CHAPTER SIX

The Flower of Prim-holistent Emptiness

VI

"*Coming Home on the Ox's Back*. The struggle is over; the man is no more concerned with gain and loss. He hums a rustic tune of the woodman, he sings simple songs of the village-boy. Saddling himself on the ox's back, his eyes are fixed on things not of the earth, earthy. Even if he is called, he will not turn his head; however enticed he will no more be kept back.

> Riding on the animal, he leisurely wends his way home:
> Enveloped in the evening mist, how tunefully the flute vanishes away!
> Singing a ditty, beating time, his heart is filled with a joy indescribable!
> That he is now one of those who know, need it be told?"

　　　　　　-from "The Ten Oxherding Pictures"
　　　　　　by Kaku-an
　　　　　　-compiled by D. T. Suzuki
　　　　　　from *Manual of Zen Buddhism*

"In the subtle level, the Soul and God unite; in the causal level, the Soul and God are both transcended in the prior identity of Godhead, or pure formless awareness, pure consciousness as such, the pure Self as pure Spirit (Atman=Brahman). No longer the "Supreme Union" of God and Soul, but the "Supreme Identity" of Godhead . . . this pure formless Spirit is said to be the Goal and Summit and Source of all manifestation. . . . In this state of formless and silent awareness, one does not *see* the Godhead, for one *is* the Godhead, and knows it from within . . . The pure Witness . . . cannot be seen, for the simple reason that it is the Seer (and the Seer itself is pure Emptiness, the pure opening or clearing in which all objects, experiences, things and events arise . . . "

-Ken Wilber
from *Sex, Ecology, Spirituality:
The Spirit of Evolution*
(See Appendix C)

"This stone (mute holds in his hand) is the Self-same Consciousness I Am."

Two ragged men sit among the trees.

The warmth of summer fills the air.

Next to them a squirrel scurries by.

Yellow and white water lilies

rest upon the pond before them.

Its surface shimmers in the sunlight.

Learned one turns to view the mute.

Seated with his back against an oak,

mute looks upon the pond in silence.

Lo: I take to mind these words you say to me,

and at the same time turn my Heart away.

I know the stone is Spirit just like You

and at the same time separate from You.

But my mind sees separation *only*.

Discrimination fills my every thought.

I hold distinction as Reality.
Still a persistent and profound fool!

I walk in shadow, in a waking dream.
A dream that's *real* in egoic terms,
with its own power, depth, substance, and form.
With its *conditional* apparency.
Like these flowering lilies on the pond,
I bob on this surface of appearance.
Through self-entrenched egoic vanity,
avarice, anger, arrogance, and lust,
self-imprisoned in this illusion realm.

This thought distinction and duality
of conception piled on conception
reveals *relative apparency*;
illusion concealing Enlightenment.

The breeze subsides and the pond is still.
Mute throws his stone into the pond.
Concentric waves spread over the pond.
Smiling, mute looks at the drifter.
Seeing the pond's surface so disturbed,
drifter looks on in deep repose.

Mute slowly fills then lights his pipe.
Learned one looks upon the pond.

A sudden breeze ripples its waters.

Brown cattails grow along its shore.

Birds of summer fill the air with song.

Drifter lies back upon the ground.

Sun and shadow play upon the leaves.

Billowing white clouds float slowly by.

Drifter closes his eyes and naps.

Soon drifter wakens and looks around.

Watching birds about, mute smokes his pipe.

Drifter now sits up next to mute.

Taking two papers from his backpack

learned one spreads these before them.

Lo: This *Tao of Emptiness* Polarity (gesturing to Figure 8).

    Flower of Prim-holistent Emptiness (continuing to gesture to Figure 8)

    from Perspective of Tao of Onliness

    as Seen through Pan-gnostic Existent eyes.

    I speak of Tao of Onliness I Ching

    and of Its Emptiness Polarity

    (pointing to the fourth-ring Yin and Yang Emptiness quadrigrams of

    Figure 4).

    These *absolute* Emptiness Realms are called

    Self of *Yang Emptiness* Enlightenment (☲)

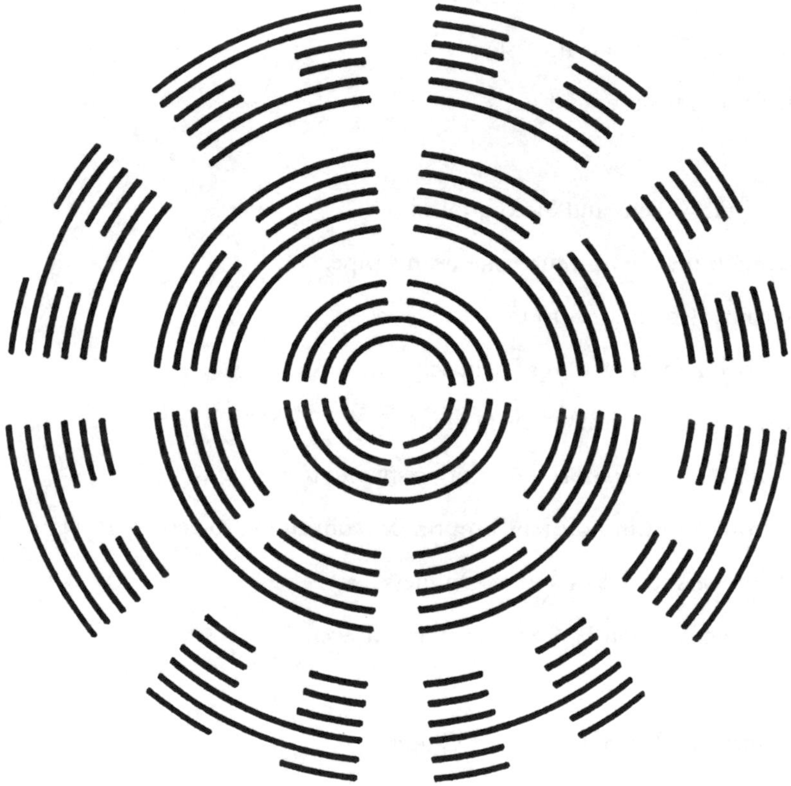

Figure 8

and *Self* of *Yin Emptiness* Enlightenment (☷),

here fused in *absolute* Polarity

(pointing respectively to these two innermost quadrigrams of Figure 8).

Two Emptiness Paths of Enlightenment

(pointing to the Yin and Yang Emptiness (☶ ☳) Realms in Figures

4 and 8).

Mute looks on the sunlit rippled pond.

Putting the large diagram away (Figure 4),

drifter takes out his photo album

and then looks down at his diagram (Figure 8).

Lo: In turn arising from, returning to

Self of Yang Emptiness Enlightenment's *absolute* Reality (☵)

(pointing to this quadrigram in Figure 8)

are these two *supreme* Realms of Emptiness:

Self of Trans-gnostic Nonbeing Emptiness (☴)

and Self of Pan-gnostic Nonbeing Emptiness (☶)

(pointing respectively to these two second-ring pentagrams in Figure 8).

Freely arising from, returning to

Self of Yin Emptiness Enlightenment's *absolute* Reality (☷)

(pointing to this quadrigram in Figure 8)

are these two *supreme* Realms of Emptiness:

Self of Pan-gnostic Being Emptiness (☱)

in greater *supreme* Polarity with

Self of Trans-gnostic Nonbeing Emptiness (☷)

(pointing respectively to these two second-ring pentagrams in Figure 8),

and Self of Trans-gnostic Being Emptiness (☵)

in lesser *supreme* Polarity with

Self of Pan-gnostic Nonbeing Emptiness (☶)

(pointing respectively to these two second-ring pentagrams in Figure 8).

Drifter appears to be deep in thought.

Picking up drifter's diagram,

mute folds it into a paper plane

and sets it sailing toward the pond.

On a breeze it glides above the pond.

Drifter scrambles into the water,

catching his paper as it floats down.

Stumbling as he walks through the mud

and holding his paper overhead,

he nearly falls into the mire,

finally emerging from the pond

covered with mud nearly to his knees.

Mute rolls in laughter on the ground.

At first drifter wears a scornful look,

but mute's laughter makes him smile.

Mute's merriment soon infects drifter,

who joins mute on the ground in laughter.

Gradually they both come to rest,

gazing up at birds and drifting clouds.

After a time both sit up again.

Learned one unfolds his paper plane,

spreading it out upon the ground.

Lo: Freely arising from, returning to

supreme Realm's Self of Pan-gnostic Nonbeing Emptiness (☷)

are two *universive* Emptiness Realms:

First, this *sixteenth* hexagram of I Ching.

In Tao of Onliness I Ching it's called

Formless Self of *Emptiness*

(pointing to this hexagram in Figure 8):

(*Formless* Self of *Emptiness*)

Here is the *image* of this hexagram

(pointing to a photo in his album) (Photo #25),

Recluse's words, its profound Voice or *text*:

> "Only Self-revelation reveal Reality."
>
> - Recluse Sage

This, its Tao of Onliness *expression*:

In singular Pan-gnostic Existence;

Emptiness awareness' trans-mental *mind-psyche* of *Reflexivity*

Emptiness meaning's *mind* of *Light*

Emptiness multiplicity's *mind* of *reflexive Fertility*

Expressed in Prim-istent Reality,

it is *Formless* Self of *Pan-gnostic Istential Emptiness*.

This *Formless* Self of Emptiness Reality (☷)

(pointing to this third-ring hexagram in Figure 8).

Second, I Ching's *thirty-fifth* hexagram.

In Tao of Onliness I Ching it's called

Boundless Self of *Emptiness*

(pointing to this hexagram in Figure 8):

(*Boundless* Self of *Emptiness*)

Here is the *image* of this hexagram

(pointing to a photo in his album) (Photo #26),

and these words are its profound Voice or *text:*

"Recognition of the SELF in its purity

is Realization of Identity with absolute Emptiness, Darkness, and Silence,

when viewed from the standpoint of relative consciousness.

In point of fact this Emptiness is Absolue Fullness

but, as such, never can be comprehended

from the perspective of egoistic consciousness."

- from *Pathways Through To Space*

by Franklin Merrell-Wolff

This, its Tao of Onliness *expression*:

In singular Pan-gnostic Existence;

Emptiness awareness' *omniscient* Consciousness

Emptiness meaning's *Perceptive mind*

Emptiness multiplicity: Radiant Sage's *mind* of *configurative Germination*

Expressed in Prim-istent Reality,

it is *Boundless* Self of *Trans-gnostic Istential Emptiness*.

This *Boundless* Self of Emptiness Reality ($\equiv\!\equiv$)

(pointing to this third-ring hexagram in Figure 8).

Both sit in silence for awhile.

With a calm face and eyes partly closed,

mute sits meditating for a time.

Finally, mute gets to his feet

and begins to slowly walk away.

Drifter gets up and walks along.

The two figures walk in dappled shade

under oak and maple canopy.

Through daisies and dandelions,

over dry leaves, twigs, and grasses,

the two walk slowly side by side.

Completely around the pond they stroll

among the thickly wooded trees

below the rustling of leaves.

Finally returning, they sit down.

Learned one lies back upon the grass,

closes his eyes and begins to nap.

Putting his cupped hands up to his mouth,

a blade of grass stretched between his thumbs,

mute blows a loud, shrill, high pitched whistle.

Startled, drifter opens his eyes wide

as if awakening from a dream.

He looks at the mute man and smiles.

A large oak tree towers above them.

Its leaves rustle in a gust of wind.

Mute packs his pipe and lights it up.

Drifter closes his eyes and soon sleeps.

After smoking, mute lies down and sleeps.

Drifter slowly wakens and sits up.

He spreads out his paper on the ground

and studies this flower diagram.

Lo: Arising from and thence returning to

supreme Realm's Self of Trans-gnostic Being Emptiness ($\equiv\equiv$)

are two *universive* Emptiness Realms:

First, this *sixty-first* I Ching hexagram.

In Tao of Onliness I Ching it's called

Divine Self of *Emptiness*

(pointing to this hexagram in Figure 8):

(*Divine* Self of *Emptiness*)

This is the *image* of this hexagram

(pointing to a photo in his album) (Photo #27),

and these words are its profound Voice or *text*:

"This (Enlightenment) is the final differentiation of Consciousness

from all forms of Consciousness,

whereupon Consciousness as Such is released in Perfect Transcendence,

which is not a transcendence from the world

but a final transcendence as the World."

-Ken Wilber

from *Eye to Eye: The Quest for the New Paradigm*

This, its Tao of Onliness *expression*:

In singular Pan-gnostic Existence;

Emptiness experience's trans-mental *heart-soul* of *Unreflexivity*

in *fundamental* Polarity with

Emptiness awareness' trans-mental *mind-psyche* of *Reflexivity*

Emptiness communion's *heart* of *Numinosity*

fused in *cardinal* Polarity with

Emptiness meaning's *mind* of *Light*

Emptiness serenity's *heart* of *unreflexive Unity*

in *elemental* Polarity with

Emptiness multiplicity's *mind* of *reflexive Fertility*

Expressed in Prim-istent Reality,

it is *Divine* Self of *Trans-gnostic Transexistential Emptiness*,

this *Divine* Self of Emptiness Reality (☵),

fused in *universive* Polarity

with *Formless* Self of *Pan-gnostic Istential Emptiness* (☶)

(pointing respectively to these two third-ring hexagrams in Figure 8).

Second, I Ching's *sixtieth* hexagram.

In Tao of Onliness I Ching it's called

Reality Self of *Emptiness*

(pointing to this hexagram in Figure 8):

(*Reality* Self of *Emptiness*)

Here is the *image* of this hexagram

(pointing to a photo in his album) (Photo #28),

and these words are its profound Voice or *text*:

"The Zen master Hakuin was praised by his neighbors as one living a pure life.

A beautiful Japanese girl whose parents owned a food store lived near him.

Suddenly, without any warning, her parents discovered she was with child.

This made her parents angry. She would not confess who the man was,

but after much harassment at last named Hakuin.

In great anger the parents went to the master.

'Is that so?' was all he would say.

After the child was born it was brought to Hakuin.

By this time he had lost his reputation, which did not trouble him,

but he took very good care of the child.

He obtained milk from his neighbors

and everything else the little one needed.

A year later the girl-mother could stand it no longer.

She told her parents the truth - that the real father of the child

was a young man who worked in the fishmarket.

The mother and father of the girl at once went to Hakuin

to ask his forgiveness, to apologize at length,

and to get the child back again.

Hakuin was willing. In yielding the child, all he said was: 'Is that so?'

-from *Zen Flesh, Zen Bones*

This, its Tao of Onliness *expression*:

In singular Pan-gnostic Existence;

Emptiness experience's *omnipotent* Consciousness

in *fundamental* Polarity with

Emptiness awareness' *omniscient* Consciousness

Emptiness communion's *Inceptive heart*

fused in *cardinal* Polarity with

Emptiness meaning's *Perceptive mind*

Emptiness serenity: Profound Sage's *heart* of *transfigurative Embrace*

in *elemental* Polarity with

Emptiness multiplicity: Radiant Sage's *mind* of *configurative Germination*

Expressed in Prim-istent Reality,

it is *Reality* Self of *Pan-gnostic Transexistential Emptiness,*

this *Reality* Self of Emptiness Reality (☷),

fused in *universive* Polarity

with *Boundless* Self of *Trans-gnostic Istential Emptiness* (☶)

(pointing respectively to these two third-ring hexagrams in Figure 8).

Drifter gets up and goes for a walk.

Hiking in the woods beyond the pond,

he stops to pick some ripe blueberries.

Returning, he takes these from his pack

along with two tuna sandwiches,

a jar of water, and some peanuts.

The two share this lunch in silence.

After clean-up they both take a nap.

Perched on a cattail at the pond,

a meadowlark sings its rhythmic tune.

Scent of this woods fills the summer air.

In awhile the mute awakens,

walks into the woods and urinates.

Drifter too wakes up as mute returns.

He sits up, stretches and looks about,

then unfolds his paper on the ground.

Lo: Likewise arising from, returning to

    supreme Realm's Self of Trans-gnostic Nonbeing Emptiness (☷)

    are two *universive* Emptiness Realms:

    First, this *forty-fifth* I Ching hexagram.

    In Tao of Onliness I Ching it's called

    Unmediated Self of *Emptiness*

    (pointing to this hexagram in Figure 8):

(*Unmediated* Self of *Emptiness*)

Here is the *image* of this hexagram
(pointing to a photo in his album) (Photo #29),
and these words are its profound Voice or *text*:

"Center of all centers, core of cores,
almond self-enclosed and growing sweet -
all this universe, to the furthest stars
and beyond them, is your flesh, your fruit.

A billion stars go spinning through the night,
blazing high above your head.
But *in* you is the presence that will be,
when all the stars are dead."

-Rainer Maria Rilke
from *The Enlightened Heart*
compiled by Stephen Mitchell

This, its Tao of Onliness *expression*:
In singular Pan-gnostic Existence;
Emptiness awareness' *boundless Gnostic mind-psyche*
Emptiness meaning's *Gnostic transcendent mind*
Emptiness multiplicity's *mind* of *meaning's Form*

Expressed in Prim-istent Reality,

it is *Unmediated* Self of *Pan-gnostic Antistential Emptiness.*

This *Unmediated* Self of Emptiness Reality (☷)

(pointing to this third-ring hexagram in Figure 8).

Second, this *twelfth* hexagram of I Ching.

In Tao of Onliness I Ching it's called

Ineffable Void Self of *Emptiness*

(pointing to this hexagram in Figure 8):

(*Ineffable Void* Self of *Emptiness*)

Here is the *image* of this hexagram

(pointing to a photo in his album) (Photo #30),

and these words are its profound Voice or *text*:

"When the nun Chiyono studied Zen under Bukko of Engaku

she was unable to attain the fruits of meditation for a long time.

At last one moonlit night she was carrying water

in an old pail bound with bamboo.

The bamboo broke and the bottom fell out of the pail,

and at that moment Chiyono was set free!

In commemoration, she wrote a poem:

In this way and that I tried to save the old pail

Since the bamboo strip was weakening and about to break

Until at last the bottom fell out.

No more water in the pail!

No more moon in the water!"

- from *Zen Flesh, Zen Bones*

This, its Tao of Onliness *expression*:

In singular Pan-gnostic Existence;

Emptiness awareness' Numinous *transparent apparency*

Emptiness meaning's *root Form of formlessness*

Emptiness multiplicity's *Comprehending mind-mirroring*

Expressed in Prim-istent Reality,

it is *Ineffable Void* Self of *Trans-gnostic Antistential Emptiness*.

This *Ineffable Void* Self of Emptiness Reality (☶)

(pointing to this third-ring hexagram in Figure 8).

Drifter looks into the sunlit woods.

Mute listens to the songs of birds

and looks up at wind-dancing leaves.

Breeze ripples water on the pond.

Lo: Sage, I Am uncreated Self of Truth

yet Comprehend and Realize It not.

I Am this boundless Awe-abyss of Truth

and yet know this only in conception.

Truly, I know the Path that I must tread.

I must let go and *die* to ego-self

so as to thus be *Born* to What I Am.

Beyond ego striving and attainment -

Knowing this Mystery of Who I Am.

But I hold back and am afraid of This.

Mute throws an acorn at the drifter,

striking him on the back of his head.

Awakened from his monologue,

drifter turns and stares at the mute.

Mute begins to laugh, then drifter too.

Drifter lies back upon the ground

and throws an acorn into the air,

trying to land it upon the mute.

Mute catches it and returns it thus.

Back and forth, they play acorn catch

until it falls out of drifter's reach.

In awhile learned one sits up

and aligns his paper before him.

Lo: Arising from and thence returning to

supreme Realm's Self of Pan-gnostic Being Emptiness (☷)

are two *universive* Emptiness Realms:

First, *forty-first* hexagram of I Ching.

In Tao of Onliness I Ching it's called

Preferenceless Self of *Emptiness*

(pointing to this hexagram in Figure 8):

(*Preferenceless* Self of *Emptiness*)

Here is the *image* of this hexagram

(pointing to a photo in his album) (Photo #31),

and these words are its profound Voice or *text*:

> "Zen students are with their masters at least ten years
>
> before they presume to teach others.
>
> Nan-in was visited by Tenno,
>
> who, having passed his apprenticeship, had become a teacher.
>
> The day happened to be rainy,
>
> so Tenno wore wooden clogs and carried the umbrella.
>
> After greeting him Nan-in remarked:
>
> 'I suppose you left your wooden clogs in the vestibule.
>
> I want to know if your umbrella is on the right or left side of the clogs.'

Tenno, confused, had no instant answer.

He realized that he was unable to carry his Zen every minute.

He became Nan-in's pupil,

and he studied six more years to accomplish his every-minute Zen."

- From *Zen Flesh, Zen Bones*

This, its Tao of Onliness *expression*:

In singular Pan-gnostic Existence;

Emptiness experience's *unconditional Gnostic heart-soul*

in *fundamental* Polarity with

Emptiness awareness' *boundless Gnostic mind-psyche*

Emptiness communion's *Gnostic transcendent heart*

fused in *cardinal* Polarity with

Emptiness meaning's *Gnostic transcendent mind*

Emptiness serenity's *heart of communion's Form*

in *elemental* Polarity with

Emptiness multiplicity's *mind* of *meaning's* Form

Expressed in Prim-istent Reality,

it is *Preferenceless* Self of *Trans-gnostic Existential Emptiness*,

this *Preferenceless* Self of Emptiness Reality (☷),

fused in *universive* Polarity

with *Unmediated* Self of *Pan-gnostic Antistential Emptiness* (☳)

(pointing respectively to these two third-ring hexagrams in Figure 8).

Second, *nineteenth* hexagram of I Ching.

In Tao of Onliness I Ching it's called

Enlightened Self of *Emptiness*

(pointing to this hexagram in Figure 8):

▬▬ ▬▬
▬▬ ▬▬
▬▬ ▬▬
▬▬▬▬▬
▬▬▬▬▬

(*Enlightened* Self of *Emptiness*)

Here is the *image* of this hexagram

(pointing to a photo in his album) (Photo #32),

and these words are its profound Voice or *text*:

> "Without opening your door,
>
> you can open your heart to the world.
>
> Without looking out your window,
>
> you can see the essence of the Tao.
>
>
> The more you know,
>
> the less you understand.
>
>
> The Master arrives without leaving,
>
> sees the light without looking,
>
> achieves without doing a thing."
>
> -Lao-tzu
>
> from *Tao Te Ching* (Stephen Mitchell Translation)

This, its Tao of Onliness *expression*:

In singular Pan-gnostic Existence;

Emptiness experience's Numinous *apparent transparency*

in *fundamental* Polarity with

Emptiness awareness' Numinous *transparent apparency*

Emptiness communion's *seed Void of emptiness*

fused in *cardinal* Polarity with

Emptiness meaning's *root Form of formlessness*

Emptiness serenity's *Apprehending heart-meditation*

in *elemental* Polarity with

Emptiness multiplicity's *Comprehending mind-mirroring*

Expressed in Prim-istent Reality,

it is *Enlightened* Self of *Pan-gnostic Existential Emptiness*,

this *Enlightened* Self of Emptiness Reality (☷),

fused in *universive* Polarity

with *Ineffable Void* Self of *Trans-gnostic Antistential Emptiness* (☰)

(pointing respectively to these two third-ring hexagrams in Figure 8).

Long shadows of afternoon appear.

Mute lies asleep upon the leaves.

Drifter looks out on the quiet pond.

A gust of wind rustles through the trees

and ripples the surface of the pond.

Mute slowly awakens and sits up.

He cleans and puts his pipe away.

They sit in silence among the trees.

The songs of birds and rustling leaves

mark the rhythm of late afternoon.

The two look out upon the pond.

Suddenly mute turns to learned one,

strikes a match and ignites his paper.

Drifter views the flame that mute has lit.

Mute picks up the flaming diagram

and holds it between their two faces.

Learned one views mute's fiery face

through his own flaming diagram.

Fire engulfs and consumes mute's face.

This reality explodes in flame.

Men, woods, pond, earth, sky; all consumed.

All of this reality vanished.

The flame alone is and remains.

Slowly it too fades and is no more.

Beyond Prim-holistent Consciousness,

This Realm, only Unmanifest, of

Arch-holistent Consciousness *Arch-ists*.

Arch-istential Arch-holistent Self.

Unfathomable, unknowable,

Arch-holistent Arch-isting "remains."

CHAPTER SEVEN

The Flower of Prim-holistent Awakening

VII

"*The Ox Forgotten, Leaving the Man Alone.* The
dharmas are one and the ox is symbolic. When you know
that what you need Is not the snare or set-net but the
hare or fish, it is liko gold separated from the dross, it is
like the moon rising out of the clouds. The one ray of
light serene and penetrating shines even before days of
creation.

> Riding on the animal, he is at last back in his home,
> Where lo! the ox is no more; the man alone sits
>   serenely.
> Though the red sun is high up in the sky, he is still
>   quietly dreaming,
> Under a straw-thatched roof are his whip and rope idly
>   lying."

-from "The Ten Oxherding Pictures"
by Kaku-an
-compiled by D. T. Suzuki
from Manual of Zen Buddhism

Through eucalyptus toward the sea
recluse woman, learned man descend.
Soon they reach the shore's precipice.
Along a path down the cliff they walk
toward the breakers of a sheltered cove.
Near the beach they pass through a ravine
and then walk onto the sandy shore.
A white sand beach lined with scattered palms,
set within this remote rock-bound cove.

Sitting on the sand against a rock,
the two look out at the breaking surf.
A warm and clear tropic mid-morning,
with a breeze blowing out to sea.
Scent of eucalyptus fills the air.

Recluse: Quester of Enlightenment,

      You are *already* That of which you seek.

Your searching is the *way* that you avoid,

creating searcher and searched-for duality.

This is conditioned and conditional knowledge.

Clinging self-possessive action dreams.

In silence, the two look out to sea.

Mountainous waves thunder as they break.

Blue ocean glistens in sunlight.

Seagulls dig in wet sand at the shore.

Learned one opens his backpack

and removes a short rod and reel,

a jar of bait, and a fish-string line.

He gets up and walks toward the sea.

On rocks projecting into the sea,

drifter baits his hook and casts his line.

Back from the shore near the ravine,

recluse woman gathers up driftwood.

She piles it next to where they sit

under a palm in this rock-lined cove.

The flounderer pulls in a flounder.

With a pocket knife he cuts this fish,

throwing head and insides to the gulls.

Meanwhile recluse lights a fire,

then sits down before it on the sand.

Learned one returns with his flounder.

Recluse looks up at him and smiles.

She wraps two potatoes in foil

taken from learned one's backpack.

Then she puts these into the fire.

Drifter wraps the fish in foil too,

then places it on a nearby rock.

Drifter turns and speaks to the recluse.

Lo: Sage, I Know I must transcend conception

if I am to Know My transcendent Self.

I must *directly* Know this Self of Truth.

Unmediated, Unconditional -

beyond ego-clinging ideation.

Now I See with my *Heart* what I must Do.

Yet I *still* step back from this Precipice.

Still a fearful, timid profound fool!

The fire burns brightly before them.

Both stare into the flame in silence.

Drifter takes two papers from his pack

and puts these on the sand before them.

Lo: *Tao of Awakening* Polarity (gesturing to Figure 9).

Prim-holistent Awakening Flower (continuing to gesture to Figure 9)

from Perspective of Tao of Onliness

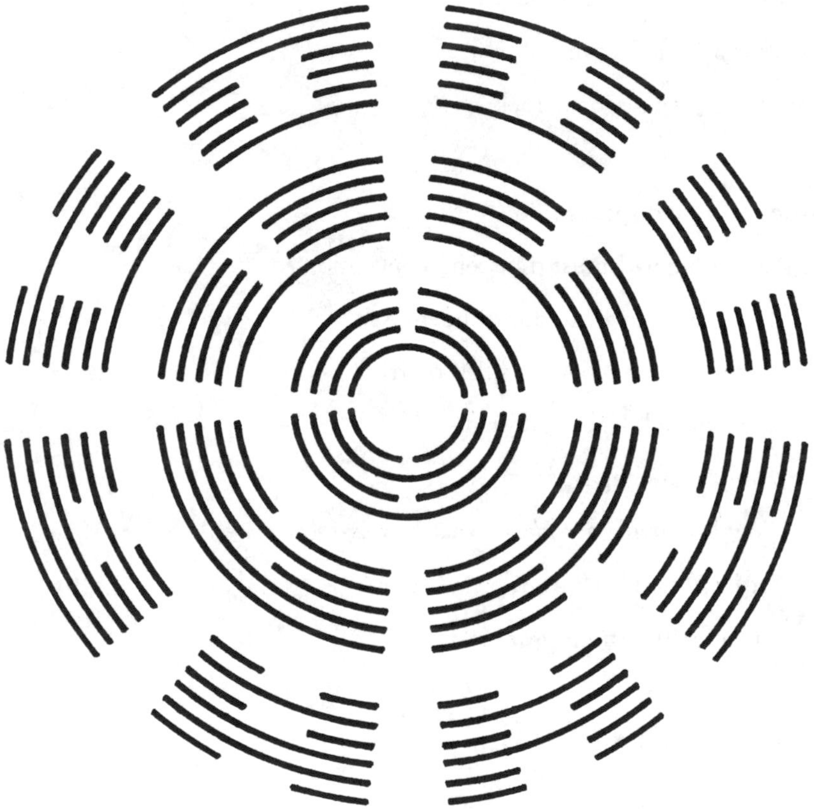

Figure 9

as Seen through Pan-gnostic Existent eyes.

This Polarity of Awakening

is of the Tao of Onliness I Ching

(pointing to the fourth-ring Yin and Yang Awakening quadrigrams of

Figure 4).

These two *absolute* Awakening Realms:

Self of *Yang Awakening* Enlightenment (☳)

and *Self* of *Yin Awakening* Enlightenment (☵),

here fused in *absolute* Polarity

(pointing respectively to these two innermost quadrigrams of Figure 9).

Raucous cries of gulls sound overhead.

Rhythmic breaking waves measure the time.

Recluse gazes into the ravine.

In the ravine, countless flowers bloom

from green and succulent ground cover.

Putting the large diagram away (Figure 4),

drifter takes out his photo album.

He views the remaining diagram (Figure 9).

Lo: Freely arising from, returning to

   Self of Yang Awakening Enlightenment's *absolute* Reality (☳)

   (pointing to this quadrigram in Figure 9)

   are two *supreme* Realms of Awakening:

Self of Trans-gnostic Nonbeing Awakening (☷)

and Self of Pan-gnostic Nonbeing Awakening (☷)

(pointing respectively to these two pentagrams in Figure 9).

Likewise arising from, returning to

Self of Yin Awakening Enlightenment's *absolute* Reality (☶ ☶)

(pointing to this quadrigram in Figure 9)

are two *supreme* Realms of Awakening:

Self of Pan-gnostic Being Awakening (☵ ☵)

in greater *supreme* Polarity with

Self of Trans-gnostic Nonbeing Awakening (☷)

(pointing respectively to these two pentagrams in Figure 9),

and Self of Trans-gnostic Being Awakening (☶ ☶)

in lesser *supreme* Polarity with

Self of Pan-gnostic Nonbeing Awakening (☷)

(pointing respectively to these two pentagrams in Figure 9).

The two sit silent for awhile.

Drifter lies back on the warm sand.

His eyes close, he listens to the surf.

Tropic morning has turned to high noon.

Recluse adds wood to the fire.

She gets up and walks along the shore.

Great breakers crash not far away.

She walks barefooted on wet sand

through waves washing her legs and feet.

Swooping gulls cry out overhead.

Drifter is asleep when she returns.

She shakes water from her legs and feet

over the chest of the learned one.

Startled, he awakens and sits up,

grabs her foot and causes her to fall.

She tumbles to the sand in laughter.

Drifter holds tight to her ankle,

but recluse easily pulls free.

Crawling on all fours upon the sand,

drifter tries to catch her but cannot.

Finally they both lie on the sand

laughing at and with each other.

Soon drifter squats before the fire.

Shifting the potatoes with a stick,

he puts the wrapped fish into the flame.

Drifter sits down before the fire

and spreads out his paper on the sand.

Lo: In turn emerging from, returning to

supreme Realm's Self of Trans-gnostic Nonbeing Awakening (☷)

are two *universive* Awakenings:

First, this *sixth* hexagram of the I Ching.

In Tao of Onliness I Ching it's called

All-pervading Self of *Awakening*

(pointing to this hexagram in Figure 9):

(*All-pervading* Self of *Awakening*)

Here is the *image* of this hexagram

(pointing to a photo in his album) (Photo #33),

and Your words are its profound Voice or *text*:

> In egoic darkness,
>
> your life passes like this gust of wind
>
> swirling and dissipating
>
> in eddies round about.
>
> You are Eternity Itself and Know It not."
>
> - Recluse Sage

This, its Tao of Onliness *expression*:

In singular Pan-gnostic Existence;

Awakening awareness' *boundless Gnostic mind-psyche*

Awakening knowledge's *psyche of all all-where Consciousness*

Awakening realization's *psyche: trans-essent, silence* of Worlds

Expressed in Prim-istent Reality,

it is *All-pervading* Self of *Trans-gnostic Antistentiul Awakening*.

This *All-pervading* Self of Awakening Reality (☰☷)

(pointing to this hexagram in Figure 9).

Next, I Ching's *forty-seventh* hexagram.

In Tao of Onliness I Ching it's called

Compassion (Sacred) Self of *Awakening*

(pointing to this hexagram in Figure 9):

(Compassion (Sacred) Self of *Awakening)*

Here is the *image* of this hexagram

(pointing to a photo in his album) (Photo #34),

and these words are its profound Voice or *text*:

> "The great Tao flows everywhere.
>
> All things are born from it,
>
> yet it doesn't create them.

It pours itself into its work,

yet it makes no claim.

It nourishes infinite worlds,

yet it doesn't hold on to them.

Since it is merged with all things

and hidden in their hearts,

it can be called humble.

Since all things vanish into it

and it alone endures,

it can be called great.

It isn't aware of its greatness;

thus it is truly great."

- from *Tao Te Ching* (Stephen Mitchell

Translation)

This, its Tao of Onliness *expression*:

In singular Pan-gnostic Existence;

Awakening awareness' Numinous *transparent apparency*

Awakening knowledge's *psyche* of *Perception*

Awakening realization's *scient psyche* of *Joy*

Expressed in Prim-istent Reality,

it is *Compassion (Sacred)* Self of *Pan-gnostic Antistential Awakening.*

This *Compassion (Sacred)* Self of Awakening Reality (☷)

(pointing to this hexagram in Figure 9).

Recluse stands up and takes off her clothes.

Drifter watches admiringly.

He too stands and removes his clothes.

Naked, they both run to the shore.

With abandon, they run round about

on the sand and into the water.

They dance about and splash each other.

In joyful play they swim and dive,

then body-surf on the breaking waves.

They laugh and howl, but say no words.

Finally, they float upon their backs

and look up to the azure sky.

These two figures walk in from the sea,

over the beach to their campfire.

Here they lie in shade on the warm sand.

Drifter looks up at the swaying palms.

Recluse rests there with her eyes closed.

The warm afternoon breeze soon dries them.

They brush sand off themselves and get dressed.

Recluse adds wood to the fire,

then sits zazen facing the rock wall.

Sounds of surf and seagulls fill the air.

For a long time no one says a word.

Drifter puts his paper on the sand

and studies his flower diagram.

Lo: Arising from and thence returning to

supreme Realm's Self of Pan-gnostic Being Awakening (☰ ☱)

are two *universive* Awakenings:

First, this *twenty-fourth* I Ching hexagram.

In Tao of Onliness I Ching it's called

Trans-manifest Self of *Awakening*

(pointing to this hexagram in Figure 9):

☷☳

(*Trans-manifest* Self of *Awakening*)

This is the *image* of this hexagram

(pointing to a photo in his album) (Photo #35),

and these words are its profound Voice or *text*:

> "In the pursuit of knowledge,
>
> every day something is added.
>
> In the practice of Tao,
>
> every day something is dropped.
>
> Less and less do you need to force things,
>
> until finally you arive at non-action.
>
> When nothing is done,
>
> nothing is left undone.

True mastery can be gained

by letting things go their own way.

It can't be gained by interfering."

- Lao-tzu from *Tao Te Ching*

Stephen Mitchell Translation

This, its Tao of Onliness *expression*:

In singular Pan-gnostic Existence;

Awakening experience's *unconditional Gnostic heart-soul*

in *fundamental* Polarity with

Awakening awareness' *boundless Gnostic mind-psyche*

Awakening compassion's *soul* of *each each-where* Consciousness

fused in *cardinal* Polarity with

Awakening knowledge's *psyche* of *all all-where* Consciousness

Awakening holiness' *soul: loving embodiment* of Worlds

in *elemental* Polarity with

Awakening realization's *psyche: trans-essent silence* of Worlds

Expressed in Prim-istent Reality,

it is *Trans-manifest* Self of *Pan-gnostic Existential Awakening*,

this *Trans-manifest* Self of Awakening Reality (☲),

fused in *universive* Polarity

with *All-pervading* Self of *Trans-gnostic Antistential Awakening* (☷)

(pointing respectively to these two hexagrams in Figure 9).

Next, *twenty-seventh* I Ching hexagram.

In Tao of Onliness I Ching it's called

Omnipresent Self of *Awakening*

(pointing to this hexagram in Figure 9):

(*Omnipresent* Self of *Awakening*)

Here is the *image* of this hexagram

(pointing to a photo in his album) (Photo #36),

and these words are its profound Voice or *text*:

"Creatures rise, creatures vanish; I alone am real, Arjuna,

looking out, amused, from deep within the eyes of every creature.

I am the Self, Arjuna, seated in the heart of every creature.

I am the origin, the middle, and the end that all must come to.

All your thoughts, all your actions, all your fears and disappointments,

offer them to me, clear-hearted; know them all as passing visions.

Thus you free yourself from bondage, from both good and evil karma;

Through your non-attachment, you embody me, in utter freedom.

Let your thoughts flow past you, calmly; keep me near, at every moment;

trust me with your life, because I *am* you, more than you yourself are."

-from *Bhagavad-Gita*

This, its Tao of Onliness *expression*:

In singular Pan-gnostic Existence;

Awakening experience's Numinous *apparent transparency*

in *fundamental* Polarity with

Awakening awareness' Numinous *transpaent apparency*

Awakening compassion's *soul* of *Inception*

fused in *cardinal* Polarity with

Awakening knowledge's *psyche* of *Perception*

Awakening holiness' *lucent soul* of *Tranquility*

in *elemental* Polarity with

Awakening realization's *scient psyche* of *Joy*

Expressed in Prim-istent Reality,

it is *Omnipresent* Self of *Trans-gnostic Existential Awakening,*

this *Omnipresent* Self of Awakening Reality (☷),

fused in *universive* Polarity

with *Compassion (Sacred)* Self of *Pan-gnostic Antistential Awakening*

(☷)

(pointing respectively to these two hexagrams in Figure 9).

Recluse woman turns from the rock wall

and looks out upon the vast ocean.

Silently they sit before the flame.

The wind has changed and a sea breeze blows.

Drifter looks up at the sunlit sea

shimmering in the warm afternoon.

Salty ocean scent is in the air.

Learned one, with a stick maneuver

takes fish and potatoes from the flame.

Recluse removes two forks, pepper, spread,

and papaya juice jar from the pack.

The two share their late lunch in silence.

After clean-up they go for a walk

along the beach to the rocky point.

Standing at this promontory's peak,

they watch breakers crash against the rocks

and listen to thundering of surf.

The breeze is gusting and stronger now.

Soon they return to their quiet place

and sit down before the dying flame.

Taking out his diagram again,

drifter places it upon the sand.

Lo: Again arising from, returning to

      supreme Realm's Self of Pan-gnostic Nonbeing Awakening (☷)

      are two *universive* Awakenings:

First, this *sixty-fourth* I Ching hexagram.

In Tao of Onliness I Ching it's called

Innate-nature Self of *Awakening*

(pointing to this hexagram in Figure 9):

(*Innate-nature* Self of *Awakening*)

Here is the *image* of this hexagram

(pointing to a photo in his album) (Photo #37),

and these words are its profound Voice or *text*:

> "Q. 'If there is no Buddhahood to be attained,
>
> has your Reverence the Buddha-function?'
>
> A. 'Where mind itself is not, whence is its functioning?'
>
> Q. 'One is then lost in outer no-ness (wu);
>
> may this not be an absolutely nihilistic view?'
>
> A. 'From the first there is (no viewer and) no viewing;
>
> and who says this to be nihilist?'
>
> Q. 'To say that from the first nothing is,
>
> is this not falling into emptiness?'
>
> A. 'Even emptiness is not, and where is the falling?'"
>
> - from *The Zen Doctrine of No-Mind*
>
> by D. T. Suzuki

This, its Tao of Onliness *expression*:

In singular Pan-gnostic Existence;

Awakening awareness' *omniscient* Consciousness

Awakening knowledge's *Gnostic transcendent psyche*

Awakening realization's *psyche* of *reflexive Clarity*

Expressed in Prim-istent Reality,

it is *Innate-nature* Self of *Trans-gnostic Istential Awakening*.

This *Innate-nature* Self of Awakening Reality (☳)

(pointing to this hexagram in Figure 9).

Second, I Ching's *fortieth* hexagram.

In Tao of Onliness I Ching it's called

Non-abiding Self of *Awakening*

(pointing to this hexagram in Figure 9):

(*Non-abiding* Self of *Awakening*)

Here is the *image* of this hexagram

(pointing to a photo in his album) (Photo #38),

and Mute's words are its profound Voice or *text*:

"Only the stilled reflective surface of this lake

Realizing itself itself, Awakens from from illusion.

But the realizations of our awakening

is yet shadow, within shadow, within shadow."

- Mute Sage

from *The Tao of Onliness: An I Ching*

Cosmology-The Awakening Years

This, its Tao of Onliness *expression*:

In singular Pan-gnostic Existence;

Awakening awareness' trans-symbolic *configurative* Self

Awakening knowledge's *psyche* of *Nonduality*

Awakening realization's *psyche* of *Resplendent*

Expressed in Prim-istent Reality,

it is *Non-abiding* Self of *Pan-gnostic Istential Awakening.*

This *Non-abiding* Self of Awakening Reality (☷)

(pointing to this hexagram in Figure 9).

Drifter lies back upon the sand.

Through palm fronds he views the vast blue sky.

He listens to gulls and breaking surf.

Recluse stretches out upon the sand,

closes her eyes and is soon asleep.

Lo: I am self-entangled in *samsara*,

self-obsessed with space-time reality.

I feel myself tied at every turn -

a prisoner of my egoic self.

I *Know* this prison as illusion too.

Know that I Am *only* Buddha-nature;

and Know that I Am *only* Christ-consciousness,

yet fear Its egoic consequences.

The two lie on the sand in silence.

Soon drifter sits up and looks about.

He unfolds his paper on the sand.

Lo: Freely arising from, returning to

    supreme Realm's Self of Trans-gnostic Being Awakening (☷)

    are two *universive* Awakenings:

    First, this *third* hexagram of the I Ching.

    In Tao of Onliness I Ching it's called

    Birthless, Deathless Self of *Awakening*

    (pointing to this hexagram in Figure 9):

(*Birthless, Deathless* Self of *Awakening*)

Here is the *image* of this hexagram

(pointing to a photo in his album) (Photo #39),

and these words are its profound Voice or *text*:

"Inwardly, no identity;

outwardly, no attachment."

- Hui-neng

from *Up From Eden* by Ken Wilber

This, its Tao of Onliness *expression*:

In singular Pan-gnostic Existence;

Awakening experience's *omnipotent* Consciousness

in *fundamental* Polarity with

Awakening awareness' *omniscient* Consciousness

Awakening compassion's *Gnostic transcendent soul*

fused in *cardinal* Polarity with

Awakening knowledge's *Gnostic transcendent psyche*

Awakening holiness' *soul of unreflexive Luminosity*

in *elemental* Polarity with

Awakening realization's *psyche* of *reflexive Clarity*

Expressed in Prim-istent Reality,

it is *Birthless, Deathless* Self of *Pan-gnostic Transexistential Awakening,*

this *Birthless, Deathless* Self of Awakening Reality (☷)

fused in *universive* Polarity

with *Innate-nature* Self of *Trans-gnostic Istential Awakening* (☶)

(pointing respectively to these two hexagrams in Figure 9).

Next, I Ching's *forty-second* hexagram.

In Tao of Onliness I Ching it's called

Wisdom (Truth) Self of *Awakening*

(pointing to this hexagram in Figure 9):

(*Wisdom (Truth)* Self of *Awakening*)

Here is the *image* of this hexagram

(pointing to a photo in his album) (Photo #40),

and Mute's words are its profound Voice or *text*:

"This sudden summer breeze,

these flickering sunlit shadows through the leaves -

Here is Enlightenment!"

- Mute Sage

This, its Tao of Onliness *expression*:

In singular Pan-gnostic Existence;

Awakening experience's trans-symbolic *transfigurative* Self

in *fundamental* Polarity with

Awakening awareness' trans-symbolic *configurative* Self

Awakening compassion's *soul* of *Eternity*

fused in *cardinal* Polarity with

Awakening knowledge's *psyche* of *Nonduality*

Awakening holiness' *soul* of *Inclusivity*

in *elemental* Polarity with

Awakening realization's *psyche* of *Resplendence*

Expressed in Prim-istent Reality,

it is *Wisdom (Truth)* Self of *Trans-gnostic Transexistential Awakening*,

this *Wisdom (Truth)* Self of Awakening Reality (☰☰),

fused in *universive* Polarity

with *Non-abiding* Self of *Pan-gnostic Istential Awakening* (☰☰)

(pointing respectively to these two hexagrams in Figure 9).

Recluse woman sleeps upon the shore.

Learned one looks out upon the sea.

Scattered billowing white clouds float by.

He looks down at embers in the flame.

Recluse awakens and sits up.

The fire's flame flickers and goes out.

Recluse woman turns to learned one.

Recluse: You struggle with many phantoms and fears.

        You must Confront *who* it is that struggles,

        and *what there is* to struggle against *what*?

Drifter looks at the glowing embers.

From her pocket recluse takes a shell;

swirling, multi-colored and cone-shaped.

Extending it over the spent flame,

she drops it into the red embers.

Instantly, the shell bursts into flame.

Fire engulfs this reality.

In an explosive swirl of flame,

man, woman, sea-cove, beach, sky, and sea -

all of this reality consumed.

The flame alone is and remains.

Slowly it too fades and is no more.

Beyond Prim-holistent Consciousness,

This Realm, only Unmanifest, of

Anti-holist Consciousness *Arch-ists*.

Arch-istent Arch-antiholist Self.

Unfathomable, unknowable,

Anti-holist Arch-isting "remains."

CHAPTER EIGHT

The Flower of Prim-holistent Mystery

VIII

"The Ox and the Man Both Gone out of Sight. All confusion is set aside, and serenity alone prevails; even the idea of holiness does not obtain. He does not linger about where the Buddha is, and as to where there is no Buddha he speedily passes by. When there exists no form of dualism, even a thousand-eyed one fails to detect a loop-hole. A holiness before which birds offer flowers is but a farce.

All is empty—the whip, the rope, the man, and the ox:
Who can ever survey the vastness of heaven?
Over the furnace burning ablaze, not a flake of snow
    can fall:
When this state of things obtains, manifest is the spirit
    of the ancient master."

-from "The Ten Oxherding Pictures"
by Kaku-an
-compiled by D. T. Suzuki
from *Manual of Zen Buddhism*

"Wanderer, Look into this Image on the lake.

This is the Face of uncreated, boundless Mystery."

Learned one leans over the water.

He hears mute's words as he bends to drink.

He looks at his facial reflection

imaged on the surface of the lake.

As if seeing it for the first time,

drifter stares intently at his face.

Then cupping up water in his hand,

he drinks from this crystal clear lake.

He turns to the mute standing nearby.

Mute looks at him without expression.

Drifter stands up and walks toward mute.

Together they walk along the beach.

Sunset illuminates the lake.

Large pines and birch grow along the shore.

Above, on embankment and hilltop,

oak trees, maple, pine, and cedar grow.

The scent of pine is in the air.

A gentle breeze blows in from the lake

slightly cooling this warm summer's eve.

Drifter and mute sit on sandy shore.

From his backpack learned one removes

some bait and a short rod and reel.

He walks over to the water's edge,

baits his hook and casts into the lake.

Mute looks out upon the glowing lake.

A jewel among dark green shadows,

still sparkling in the dying light.

Soon drifter pulls in a large-mouth bass.

He takes it to a nearby log

and filets it with his pocket knife,

leaving the rest for hungry raccoons.

Drifter puts his fishing gear away.

Meanwhile mute walks along the beach

stopping now and then to look about.

The two walk up the embankment path

to their quiet place upon the hill.

Once atop the hill Mute gathers wood,

piling it near to where they sit

at the hill's crest in view of the lake.

Twilight sky reflects upon the lake.

To the West, black pines silhouetted

against a peach and amber sky.

A loon's long cry spreads over the lake.

While learned one starts a fire,

mute wraps the fish and two potatoes

in foil taken from drifter's pack.

Setting the wrapped filets aside,

he puts the potatoes in the flame.

The two sit before the fire

and look out upon the twilit lake.

Waters ripple crimson and purple.

Whisper of waves lap upon the shore.

Scent of burning wood now fills the air.

Near-full moon is rising through the pines.

They sit zazen, meditating there.

After a long while drifter speaks.

Lo: World-honored One, thank you for Your words.

     So far am I removed from my own Self!

     So distant, this egoic life of mine

from the Suchness of My eternal Face.

Still, I hold to egoic existence

like a beggar guarding a scrap of bread.

I Know that this must all come to an end.

I must Release myself unto Myself

through effortless and meritless No-mind.

A whippoorwill sings its evening song.

Learned one looks out across the lake.

Mute lies back and stretches on the grass.

Drifter takes two papers from his pack

and puts these on the ground before him.

Lo: This *Tao of Mystery* Polarity (gesturing to Figure 10).

Flower of Prim-holistent Mystery (continuing to gesture to Figure 10)

from Perspective of Tao of Onliness

as Seen through Pan-gnostic Existent eyes.

I speak of Tao of Onliness I Ching

and of Its Mystery Polarity

(pointing to the fourth-ring Yin and Yang Mystery quadrigrams of

Figure 4).

These *absolute* Mystery Realms are called

Self of *Yang Mystery* Enlightenment (☲)

and *Self* of *Yin Mystery* Enlightenment (☵),

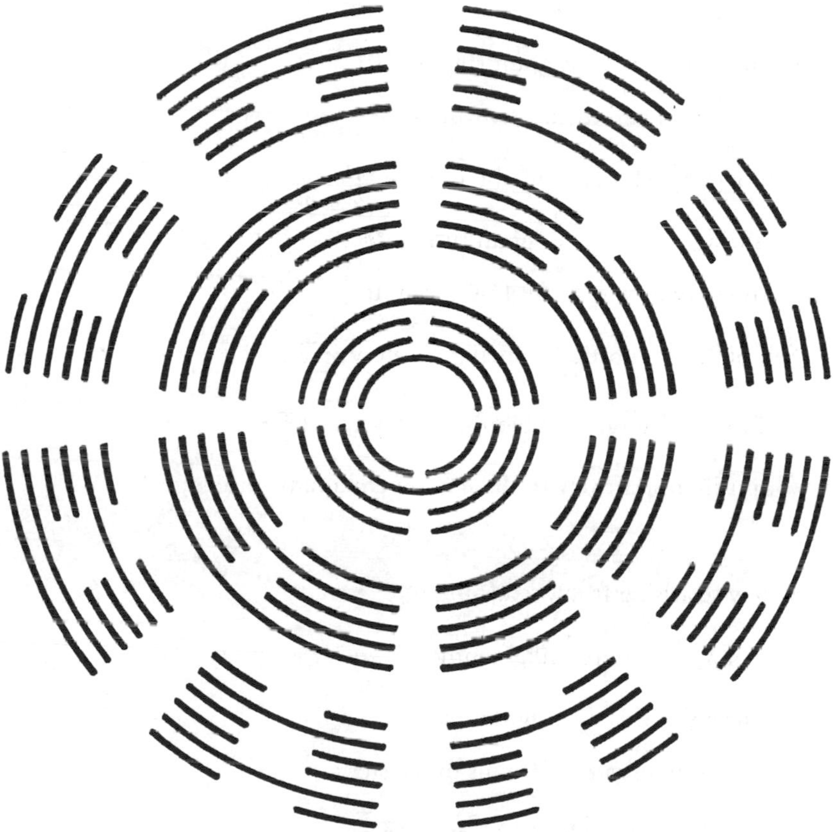

Figure 10

here fused in *absolute* Polarity

(pointing respectively to these two innermost quadrigrams of Figure 10).

Putting the large diagram away (Figure 4),

drifter takes out his photo album.

Mute lies asleep upon the grass.

Drifter views his flower diagram (Figure 10).

Lo: Arising from and thence returning to

Self of Yang Mystery Enlightenment's *absolute* Reality (☷)

(pointing to this quadrigram in Figure 10)

are these two *supreme* Realms of Mystery:

Self of Trans-gnostic Nonbeing Mystery (☵)

and Self of Pan-gnostic Nonbeing Mystery (☶)

(pointing respectively to these two pentagrams in Figure 10).

Likewise arising from, returning to

Self of Yin Mystery Enlightenment's *absolute* Reality (☳)

(pointing to this quadrigram in Figure 10)

are these two *supreme* Realms of Mystery:

Self of Pan-gnostic Being Mystery (☱)

in greater *supreme* Polarity with

Self of Trans-gnostic Nonbeing Mystery (☴)

(pointing respectively to these two pentagrams in Figure 10),

and Self of Trans-gnostic Being Mystery (☲)

in lesser *supreme* Polarity with

Self of Pan-gnostic Nonbeing Mystery ($\equiv\ \equiv$)

(pointing respectively to these two pentagrams in Figure 10).

Night has fallen and the lake is dark.
Drifter adds more wood to the fire,
then shifts the potatoes with a stick.
Sparks rise from the flame into the night.
The breeze subsides and the lake is still.

The moon ascends over the lake.
Drifter looks into the dancing flame.
Mute awakens, stretches and sits up.
Arising, mute yawns and looks about.
He walks down the path and to the beach.
Soon drifter gets up and follows him.

Mute removes his shoes and all his clothes
and walks into the moonlit lake.
Learned one also starts to undress.
Mute turns back and splashes the drifter
whose pants are still not completely off.
Drifter runs, but trips upon his pants
and falls face first upon the sand.
The naked mute howls with laughter
and dances in the shallow water.

At first drifter is not much amused,

but soon he is laughing with the mute

and dancing naked on the beach.

In the warm lake they dive and swim.

They howl and laugh and splash about.

Both swim out and float upon their backs,

and gaze up at billowed moonlit clouds.

Finally, they both return to shore.

The two sit down on the sandy beach

and soon the breeze dries both of them.

They brush sand from themselves and get dressed.

Both walk up the path to the hilltop.

Mute puts more wood upon the fire,

then puts the wrapped fish into the flame.

Learned one spreads out his diagram.

Lo: Freely arising from, returning to

  supreme Realm's Self of Pan-gnostic Nonbeing Mystery (☳)

  are two *universive* Mystery Realms:

  First, this *fifty-first* I Ching hexagram.

  In Tao of Onliness I Ching it's called

  Consciousness Self of *Mystery*

  (pointing to this hexagram in Figure 10):

(*Consciousness* Self of *Mystery*)

Here is the *image* of this hexagram

(pointing to a photo in his album) (Photo #41),

and these words are its profound Voice or *text*:

"When Banzan was walking through a market

he overheard a conversation between a butcher and his customer.

'Give me the best piece of meat you have,' said the customer.

'Everything in my shop is the best,' replied the butcher.

'You cannot find here any piece of meat that is not the best.'

At these words Banzan became enlightened."

-from *Zen Flesh, Zen Bones*

compiled by Paul Reps

This, its Tao of Onliness *expression*:

In singular Pan-gnostic Existence;

Mystery experience's trans-mental *heart-soul* of *Unreflexivity*

Mystery compassion's *soul* of *Transfiguration*

Mystery holiness' *soul* of *compassion's Form*

Expressed in Prim-istent Reality,

it is *Consciousness* Self of *Pan-gnostic Istential Mystery*.

This *Consciousness* Self of Mystery Reality (⚏)

(pointing to this hexagram in Figure 10).

Second, I Ching's *twenty-first* hexagram.

In Tao of Onliness I Ching it's called

Alpha and Omega Self of *Mystery*

(pointing to this hexagram in Figure 10):

(*Alpha and Omega* Self of *Mystery*)

Here is the *image* of this hexagram

(pointing to a photo in his album) (Photo #42),

and these words are its profound Voice or *text*:

> "He who finds it (Brahman, Self, Atman) is free;
>
> he has found himself; he has solved the great riddle;
>
> his heart forever is at peace.
>
> Whole, he enters the Whole.
>
> His personal self returns to its radiant, intimate, deathless source.
>
> As rivers lose name and form when they disappear into the sea,
>
> the sage leaves behind all traces
>
> when he disappears into the light.

Perceiving the truth, he becomes the truth;

he passes beyond all suffering, beyond death;

all the knots of his heart are loosed."

-from *The Upanishads*

quoted in *The Enlightened Heart*

This, its Tao of Onliness *expression*:

In singular Pan-gnostic Existence;

Mystery experience's *power* of *trans-ceptive Boundlessness*

Mystery compassion's *soul* of *boundless Vergency*

Mystery holiness' *soul* of *each all-where Receptivity*

Expressed in Prim-istent Reality,

it is *Alpha and Omega* Self of *Trans-gnostic Istential Mystery*.

This *Alpha and Omega* Self of Mystery Reality (☲)

(pointing to this hexagram in Figure 10).

Gentle gusts of wind blow from the lake.

Scent of pine and lake ride on the breeze.

Learned one adds wood to the fire.

Mute looks out upon the moonlit lake

glittering and rippled by the wind.

Silently they sit before the flame.

Mute lies back upon the grass of earth

and gazes up at the star-filled sky.

Soon his eyes close and he falls asleep.

Drifter looks down at his diagram.

Lo: Emerging from and thence returning to

supreme Realm's Self of Trans-gnostic Being Mystery (⚏)

are two *universive* Mystery Realms:

First, this *fifty-ninth* I Ching hexagram.

In Tao of Onliness I Ching it's called

Pathless Self of *Mystery*

(pointing to this hexagram in Figure 10):

(Pathless Self of *Mystery)*

Here is the *image* of this hexagram

(pointing to a photo in his album) (Photo #43),

and these words are its profound Voice or *text*:

"Hyakujo wished to send a monk to open a new monastery.

He told his pupils that whoever answered a question most ably

would be appointed.

Placing a water vase on the ground, he asked:

'Who can say what this is without calling its name?'

The chief monk said: 'No one can call it a wooden shoe.'

Isan, the cooking monk, tipped over the vase with his foot and went out.

Hyakujo smiled and said: 'The chief monk loses.'

And Isan became the master of the new monastery.

Mumon's comment: Isan was brave enough,

but he could not escape Hyakujo's trick.

After all, he gave up a light job and took a heavy one.

Why, can't you see, he took off his comfortable hat

and placed himself in iron stocks.

Giving up cooking utensils,

Defeating the chatterbox,

Though his teacher sets a barrier for him

His feet will tip over everything, even the Buddha

-from *Zen Flesh, Zen Bones*

This, its Tao of Onliness *expression*:

In singular Pan-gnostic Existence;

Mystery awareness' trans-mental *mind-psyche* of *Reflexivity*

in *fundamental* Polarity with

Mystery experience's trans-mental *heart-soul* of *Unreflexivity*

Mystery knowledge's *psyche* of *Configuration*

fused in *cardinal* Polarity with

Mystery compassion's *soul* of *Transfiguration*

Mystery realization: *psyche* of *knowledge's Form*

in *elemental* Polarity with

Mystery holiness: *soul* of *compassion's Form*

Expressed in Prim-istent Reality,

it is *Pathless* Self of *Trans-gnostic Transexistential Mystery*,

this *Pathless* Self of Mystery Reality (☷),

fused in *universive* Polarity

with *Consciousness* Self of *Pan-gnostic Istential Mystery* (☶)

(pointing respectively to these two hexagrams in Figure 10).

Second, I Ching's *twenty-ninth* hexagram.

In Tao of Onliness I Ching it's called

Liberated Self of *Mystery*

(pointing to this hexagram in Figure 10):

(*Liberated* Self of *Mystery*)

Here is the *image* of this hexagram

(pointing to a photo in his album) (Photo #44),

and these words are its profound Voice or *text*:

"Two monks were arguing about a flag.

One said: 'The flag is moving.' The other said: 'The wind is moving.'

The six patriarch happened to be passing by.

He told them: 'Not the wind, not the flag; mind is moving.'

Mumon's comment: The sixth patriarch said:

'The wind is not moving, the flag is not moving.

Mind is moving.' What did he mean? If you understand this intimately,

you will see the two monks there trying to buy iron and gaining gold.

The sixth patriarch could not bear to see those two dull heads,

so he made such a bargain.

Wind, flag, mind moves,

The same understanding.

When the mouth opens

All is wrong.

-from *Zen Flesh, Zen Bones*

This, its Tao of Onliness *expression*:

In singular Pan-gnostic Existence;

Mystery awareness's *vision of holo-ceptive Unconditionality*

in *fundamental* Polarity with

Mystery experience's *power of trans-ceptive Boundlessness*

Mystery knowledge's *psyche of unconditional Convergency*

fused in *cardinal* Polarity with

Mystery compassion's *soul of boundless Vergency*

Mystery realization's *psyche of all each-where Radiance*

in *elemental* Polarity with

Mystery holiness' *soul of each all-where Receptivity*

Expressed in Prim-istent Reality,

it is *Liberated* Self of *Pan-gnostic Transexistential Mystery*,

this *Liberated* Self of Mystery Reality (☷),

fused in *universive* Polarity

with *Alpha and Omega* Self of *Trans-gnostic Istential Mystery* (☶)

(pointing respectively to these two hexagrams in Figure 10).

Drifter looks out upon the night lake.

Its waters shimmer in the moonlight.

Mute stirs, awakens and sits up.

From the pack mute takes out two peaches,

jar of prune juice, pepper, forks, and spread.

Learned one, with a stick maneuver,

takes fish and potatoes from the flame.

The two share this repast in silence.

Savory aromas fill the air.

After clean-up mute lights up his pipe.

A gust of wind ripples on the lake,

passing to the shore and up the hill.

The flame flares and swirls in the wind.

Night wind whispers through the giant pines.

Drifter puts his paper on the grass.

Lo: Sage, arising from and returning to

supreme Realm's Self of Trans-gnostic Nonbeing Mystery (☳)

are two *universive* Mystery Realms:

First, this *seventeenth* I Ching hexagram.

In Tao of Onliness I Ching it's called

Ecstatic Realization Self of *Mystery*

(pointing to this hexagram in Figure 10):

(*Ecstatic Realization* Self of *Mystery*)

Here is the *image* of this hexagram

(pointing to a photo in his album) (Photo #45),

Recluse's words, its profound Voice or *text*:

> "The Wind of Illumination
> blows everywhere and nowhere *all* the same.
> Vagabond, See Me *beyond* shadows.
> Know Me as the *Truth* I Am.
> I Am Illumination's Wind.
> Hear My silent Words.
> Birthless, Deathless, Boundless, and Unconditional,
> I Am *Reality*.
>
> -Recluse Sage

This, its Tao of Onliness *expression*:

In singular Pan-gnostic Existence;

Mystery experience's *genesis* of *Creativity*

Mystery compassion's *soul* of *Presence*

Mystery holiness' *apprehending body* of *Love*

Expressed in Prim-istent Reality,

it is *Ecstatic Realization* Self of *Pan-gnostic Antistential Mystery*.

This *Ecstatic Realization* Self of Mystery Reality (☲)

(pointing to this hexagram in Figure 10).

Second, *twenty-fifth* I Ching hexagram.

In Tao of Onliness I Ching it's called

Universal Self of *Mystery*

(pointing to this hexagram in Figure 10):

(*Universal* Self of *Mystery*)

Here is the *image* of this hexagram

(pointing to a photo in his album) (Photo #46),

and these words are its profound Voice or *text*:

"My daily affairs are quite ordinary;

but I'm in total harmony with them.

I don't hold on to anything, don't reject anything;

nowhere an obstacle or conflict.

Who cares about wealth or honor?

Even the poorest thing shines.

My miraculous power and spiritual activity:

drawing water and carrying wood."

-Layman P'ang

from *The Enlightened Heart*

compiled by Stephen Mitchell

This, its Tao of Onliness *expression*:

In singular Pan-gnostic Existence;

Mystery experience's *Void* of *eternity*

Mystery compassion's *soul* of *Receptivity*

Mystery holiness: Holy Sage's *soul* of *transfigurative Grace*

Expressed in Prim-istent Reality,

it is *Universal* Self of *Trans-gnostic Antistential Mystery*.

This *Universal* Self of Mystery Reality (☷)

(pointing to this hexagram in Figure 10).

Mute puts more wood upon the fire.

Drifter stands up and looks about,

walks into the woods and urinates.

He returns and sits before the flame.

A cooler breeze blows in from the lake.

Lo: How deeply rooted is egoic self!

How tenacious, fierce, and entrenched it is!

This integrative insight and power.

Ego's *towering* rationality

and profound language and artistic sense.

This great painter of self reality.

I See this striving self of which I am.

See ego mind as one aspect of Self

and not the final self it seems to be.

Mute lies back and looks up at the pines

silhouetted in the moonlit sky.

Drifter watches shadows in the trees

cast by the firelight passing through.

He turns to his paper on the ground.

Lo: Arising from and thence returning to

   supreme Realm's Self of Pan-gnostic Being Mystery (☷)

   are two *universive* Mystery Realms:

First, this *fourth* hexagram of the I Ching.

In Tao of Onliness I Ching it's called

All-encompassing Self of *Mystery*

(pointing to this hexagram in figure 10):

```
▬▬▬▬▬▬▬
▬▬   ▬▬
▬▬▬▬▬▬▬
▬▬   ▬▬
▬▬   ▬▬
▬▬   ▬▬
```

(*All-encompassing* Self of *Mystery*)

Here is the *image* of this hexagram
(pointing to a photo in his album) (Photo #47),
and these words are its profound Voice or *text*:

"United with Brahman, cut free from the fruit of the act,

A man finds peace in the work of the spirit.

Without Brahman, man is a prisoner,

Enslaved by action, dragged onward by desire.

Happy is the dweller in the city of nine gates (the human body)

Whose discrimination has cut him free from his act:

He is not involved in action, he does not involve others.

Do not say: 'God gave us this delusion.'

You dream you are the doer, you dream that action is done,

You dream that action bears fruit.

It is your ignorance, it is the world's delusion

That gives you these dreams."

-from *Bhagavad-Gita*

This, its Tao of Onliness *expression*:

In singular Pan-gnostic Existence;

Mystery awareness' *morphosis* of *Productivity*

in *fundamental* Polarity with

Mystery experience's *genesis* of *Creativity*

Mystery knowledge's *psyche* of *Silence*

fused in *cardinal* Polarity with

Mystery compassion's *soul* of *Presence*

Mystery realization's *comprehending seed* of *Vision*

in elemental Polarity with

Mystery holiness' *apprehending body* of *Love*

Expressed in Prim-istent Reality,

it is *All-encompassing* Self of *Trans-gnostic Existential Mystery*,

this *All-encompassing* Self of Mystery Reality (☷),

fused in *universive* Polarity

with *Ecstatic Realization* Self of *Pan-gnostic Antistential Mystery* (☴)

(pointing respectively to these two hexagrams in Figure 10).

Second, this *seventh* I Ching hexagram.

In Tao of Onliness I Ching it's called

Identity Self of *Mystery*

(pointing to this hexagram in figure 10):

▬▬ ▬▬
▬▬ ▬▬
▬▬ ▬▬
▬▬ ▬▬
▬▬▬▬▬
▬▬ ▬▬

(*Identity* Self of *Mystery*)

Here is the *image* of this hexagram

(pointing to a photo in his album) (Photo #48),

and these words are its profound Voice or *text*:

" 'What are we really doing don Juan?' I asked

'Is it possible that warriors are only preparing themselves for death?'

'No way,' he said, gently patting my shoulder.

'Warriors prepare themselves to be aware,

and full awareness comes to them

only when there is no more self-importance left in them.

Only when they are nothing do they become everything.' "

-from *The Fire From Within*

by Carlos Castaneda

This, its Tao of Onliness *expression*:

In singular Pan-gnostic Existence;

Mystery awareness' *Form* of *nonduality*

in *fundamental* Polarity with

Mystery experience's *Void* of *eternity*

Mystery knowledge's *psyche* of *Stillness*

fused in *cardinal* Polarity with

Mystery compassion's *soul* of *Receptivity*

Mystery realization: Joyful Sage's *psyche* of *configurative Beauty*

in *elemental* Polarity with

Mystery holiness: Holy sage's *soul* of *transfigurative Grace*

Expressed in Prim-istent Reality,

it is *Identity* Self of *Pan-gnostic Existential Mystery,*

this *Identity* Self of Mystery Reality (☷),

fused in *universive* Polarity

with *Universal* Self of *Trans-gnostic Antistential Mystery* (☶)

(pointing respectively to these two hexagrams in Figure 10).

Mute lies asleep upon the ground.

Learned one looks out across the lake.

An owl is hooting in the woods.

The fire is slowly dying out.

Scent of smoking embers fills the air.

Drifter looks into the dying flame.

The breeze subsides and there is silence.

Mute awakens, stretches and sits up.

He picks up his peach seed from supper

and tosses it into the fire.

Instantly, the seed bursts into flame.

Fire engulfs this reality.

In one vast ferocious inferno,

the two men, hill, woods, shore, lake, and sky -

all of this reality consumed.

The flame alone is and remains.

Slowly it too fades and is no more.

Beyond Arch-istential Consciousness,

This Realm, only Unmanifest, of

Omni-holist Consciousness *Omnists*.

Omnistent Omni-holistent Self.

Unfathomable, unknowable,

Omni-holist Omnisting "remains."

CHAPTER NINE

The Flower of Prim-holistent Mind

IX

"Returning to the Origin, Back to the Source. From the
very beginning, pure and immaculate, the man has never
been affected by defilement. He watches the growth of
things, while himself abiding in the immovable serenity of
non-assertion. He does not identify himself with the
maya-like transformations [that are going on about him],
nor has he any use of himself [which is artificiality]. The
waters are blue, the mountains are green; sitting alone,
he observes things undergoing changes.

> To return to the Origin, to be back at the Source—
>   already a false step this!
> Far better it is to stay at home, blind and deaf, and
>   without much ado;
> Sitting in the hut, he takes no cognisance of things
>   outside,
> Behold the streams flowing—whither nobody knows;
>   and the flowers vividly red—for whom are they?"
>   -from "The Ten Oxherding Pictures"
>   by Kaku-an
>   -compiled by D. T. Suzuki
>   from *Manual of Zen Buddhism*

231

Over foothills rising from the sea,

through deep ravines and on steep inclines,

up the mountain the two figures climb.

Past waterfalls and high walls of rock,

mute and recluse climb 'til almost noon.

Two figures alone in wilderness.

Lush tropic growth blankets the mountain

which overlooks the expansive sea.

A seabreeze blows and the sky is clear.

Flowers bloom throughout the mountainside.

Near the top they find a mountain stream

cascading in rock-lined waterfalls

into successive crystal pools.

At one pool drifter stops to drink.

Recluse sits down on grass-covered ground

in the shelter of this rock-bound cove.

Soon drifter joins her on the grass.

A cedar tree shades them from the sun.

Water flows and plays a splashing song.

Both move over to the steep rock wall.

Full-lotus, facing this rock wall,

they sit zazen and meditate.

In an hour they sit on the grass

facing the waterfall and pool.

Recluse points to the flowing water.

Recluse: Slayer of phantoms, see this ripple on the stream?

This is your space-time mind-body *self* of consciousness.

This whole/part holonic ego *self.* (Wilber, 1995)

Just like this ripple of the stream,

the mind-body *self* appears, evolves, and disappears.

But the Water of Consciousness of which this ripple is,

is Seamless, Boundless, and Unconditional,

even as It Manifests *this* way of rippling.

Awakening gypsy, *You* are this ripple apparency

and the birthless, deathless Water of the Stream.

Learned one looks at the distant sea.

Recluse lies back and closes her eyes.

Lo: World-honored One, thank you for Your words,

yet I remain a dunce in many ways.

Still much obsessed with my cosmology

and its myriad conceptual schemes.

But also loosening egoic ties

and for brief moments glimpsing Who I Am,

if only from a distance far removed.

Primarily I lead my ego life;

petty, clinging, self-conscious, self-absorbed.

Yet as my meditation grows deeper,

I Come to Know greater and greater Bliss;

a 'peace that passeth all understanding.'

I come to *See* this *Self* of *Who I Am*

beyond this mind-body of ego life.

Sunlight of early afternoon

glistens on the ocean far below.

Drifter looks down on this lush green land

cut by towering gray walls of stone.

Then he looks out on the vast blue sea.

For a long time he sits silent so.

Drifter takes two papers from his pack

and puts these on the grass before him.

Lo: Sage, this is *Tao of Mind* Polarity (gesturing to Figure 11).

This Flower of Prim-holistential Mind (continuing to gesture to Figure 11)

from Perspective of Tao of Onliness

as Seen through Pan-gnostic Existent eyes.

I speak of Tao of Onliness I Ching

and Its transcendent Mind Polarity

(pointing to the fourth-ring Yin and Yang Mind quadrigrams of Figure 4).

Self of *Yang Mind* Enlightenment (☰)

and *Self* of *Yin Mind* Enlightenment (☷)

are the Names of These *absolute* Mind Realms

here fused in *absolute* Polarity

(pointing respectively to these two innermost quadrigrams of Figure 11).

Putting the large diagram away (Figure 4),

drifter takes out his photo album.

Recluse opens her eyes and sits up.

Scent of wild flowers float on winds

gusting from the deep ravines below.

Recluse looks toward the mountain top

and at white clouds passing over it.

Drifter looks down at his diagram.

Lo: In turn arising from, returning to

Self of Yang Mind Enlightenment's *absolute* Reality (☰)

(pointing to this quadrigram in Figure 11)

are two *supreme* Realities of Mind:

Self of Trans-gnostic Nonbeing Mind (☰)

and Self of Pan-gnostic Nonbeing Mind (☳)

(pointing respectively to these two pentagrams in Figure 11).

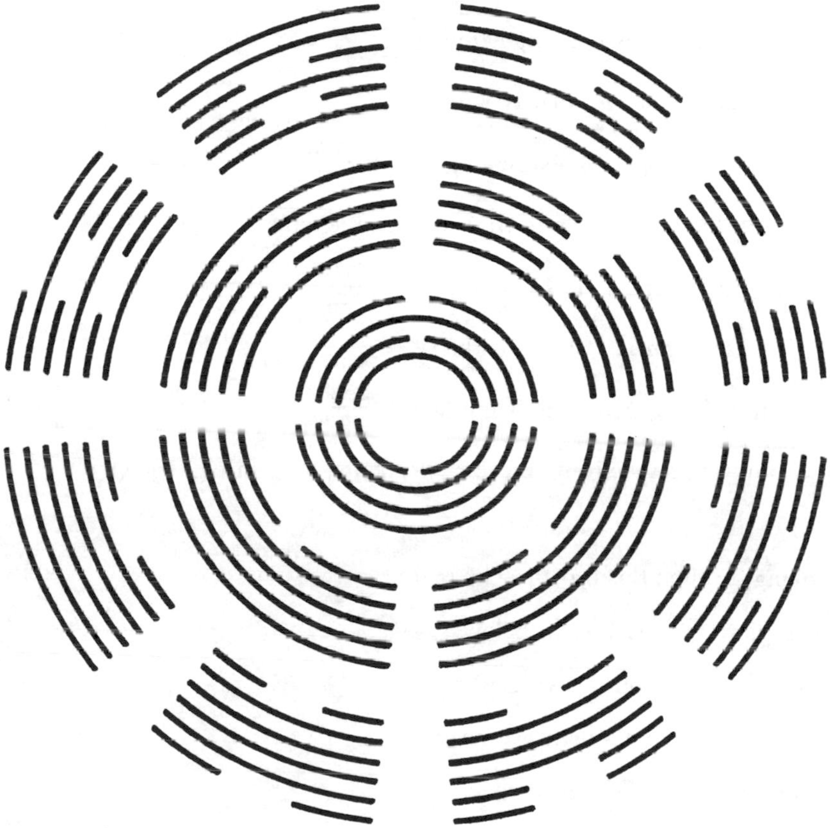

Figure 11

Likewise arising from, returning to

Self of Yin Mind Enlightenment's *absolute* Reality (☶)

(pointing to this quadrigram in Figure 11)

are two *supreme* Realities of Mind:

Self of Pan-gnostic Being Mind (☷)

in greater *supreme* Polarity with

Self of Trans-gnostic Nonbeing Mind (☴)

(pointing respectively to these two pentagrams in Figure 11),

and Self of Trans-gnostic Being Mind (☵)

in lesser *supreme* Polarity with

Self of Pan-gnostic Nonbeing Mind (☳)

(pointing respectively to these two pentagrams in Figure 11).

Looking through this broad rocky ravine
drifter views the seacliffs far below.
Recluse looks out on the windswept sea.
The tropic sun shines high overhead.
Arising, recluse walks out of view.
She returns and sits upon the grass.

Drifter looks into the clear pool.
Light and shade dance on its calm surface.
Recluse takes off her shoes and socks,
then wades into the crystal pool.

She splashes water on drifter,

some of which falls on his diagram.

Startled, he looks at the recluse,

then sweeps the water from his paper.

Recluse laughs uproariously,

but slips and sits down in the water.

Now both laugh uncontrollably.

Recluse and drifter both undress.

Recluse sits under the waterfall.

The water cascades over her head

covering her face like a vail.

Naked, drifter wades in the pool.

The two engage in a splashing fight,

wildly dousing one another.

Soon tired, they sit in the pool.

Recluse looks out on the far blue sea

glistening in sunlit afternoon.

Drifter looks into the clear water

at the black rockbed of the pool.

Early turns to mid afternoon.

Recluse woman floats upon her back

looking at white clouds and the blue sky.

Drifter stands under the waterfall

watching recluse float upon her back.

Lying in the sun upon the grass,

they soon dry in the summer breeze.

Birds fly and clouds float overhead.

Wind whispers through the cedar branches.

The scent of cedar is in the air.

Learned man and recluse woman dress.

She climbs up and sits upon a rock

and looks out upon the sunlit sea.

He lies on the grass with his eyes closed.

Learned one sits up as she returns.

He lays down his paper on the grass.

Lo: Freely arising from, returning to

   supreme Realm's Self of Trans-gnostic Nonbeing Mind (☰)

   are these two *universive* Realms of Mind:

First, this *forty-fourth* I Ching hexagram.

In Tao of Onliness I Ching it's called

Nameless, Not Even Self of *Mind*

(pointing to this hexagram in Figure 11):

(*Nameless, Not Even* Self of *Mind*)

Here is the *image* of this hexagram
(pointing to a photo in his album) (Photo #49),
and these words are its profound Voice or *text*:

"Marvelous! Marvelous!
All beings are already enlightened!
It is only because of their delusions
that they don't realize this."

-Buddha

from *The Enlightened Mind*

compiled by Stephen Mitchell

This, its Tao of Onliness *expression*:
In singular Pan-gnostic Existence;
Mind awareness' *Form* of *nonduality*
Mind knowledge's *Holo-scient psyche*
Mind intuition: Quiet Sage's *psyche* of *configurative Fluidity*

Expressed in Prim-istent Reality,
it is *Nameless, Not Even* Self of *Trans-gnostic Antistential Mind*.

This *Nameless, Not Even* Self of Mind Reality (☰̄)

(pointing to this hexagram in Figure 11).

Second, *twenty-eighth* I Ching hexagram.

In Tao of Onliness I Ching it's called

Buddha-nature Self of *Mind*

(pointing to this hexagram in Figure 11):

(*Buddha-nature* Self of *Mind*)

Here is the *image* of this hexagram

(pointing to a photo in his album) (Photo #50),

and these words are its profound Voice or *text*:

> "His heart is with Brahman,
>
> His eyes in all things
>
> Sees only Brahman
>
> Equally present,
>
> Knows his own Atman
>
> In every creature,
>
> All all creation
>
> Within that Atman."
>
> -from *Bhagavad-Gita*
>
> Swami Prahavananda and Christopher

Isherwood Translation

This, its Tao of Onliness *expression*:

In singular Pan-gnostic Existence;

Mind awareness' *vision* of *holo-ceptive Unconditionality*

Mind knowledge *psyche* of *Morphosis*

Mind intuition's *psyche* of *Through-ness reflexivity*

Expressed in Prim-istent Reality,

it is *Buddha-nature* Self of *Pan-gnostic Antistential Mind.*

This *Buddha-nature* Self of Mind Reality (☰)

(pointing to this hexagram in Figure 11).

Recluse views ripples on the pool

glittering in afternoon sunlight.

Drifter looks upon a far seacliff

and surf crashing on its rocky shores.

Both sit meditating for a time.

Drifter takes a box from his backpack.

From it he takes *I Ching*, wrapped in cloth

also fifty foot-long bamboo sticks.

Learned one consults the *Book of Change.*

Gusts of wind stream up the broad ravine.

Recluse lies back upon the ground

and looks up at passing clouds and sky.

Drifter views his flower diagram.

Lo: Arising from and thence returning to

supreme Realm's Self of Pan-gnostic Being Mind (☷)

are these two *universive* Realms of Mind:

First, this *thirty-sixth* I Ching hexagram.

In Tao of Onliness I Ching it's called

Abyss Self of *Mind*

(pointing to this hexagram in Figure 11):

☷
☳

(*Abyss* Self of *Mind*)

Here is the *image* of this hexagram

(pointing to a photo in his album) (Photo #51),

and Mute's words are its profound Voice or *text*:

"This is the Water of Consciousness.

Drinking from this Wellspring

We quench Our Thirst of Consciousness.

Likewise, We are the Water of the Wellspring It Drinks from,

and Its quenched Thirst of Consciousness."

-Mute Sage

This, its Tao of Onliness *expression*:

In singular Pan-gnostic Existence;

Mind experience's *Void* of *eternity*

in *fundamental* Polarity with

Mind awareness' *Form* of *nonduality*

Mind compassion's *Translucent soul*

fused in *cardinal* Polarity with

Mind knowledge's *Holo-scient psyche*

Mind righteousness: Vital Sage's *soul* of *transfigurative Intensity*

in *elemental* Polarity with

Mind intuition: Quiet Sage's *psyche* of *configurative Fluidity*

Expressed in Prim-istent Reality,

it is *Abyss* Self of *Pan-gnostic Existential Mind,*

this *Abyss* Self of Mind Reality (☷),

fused in *universive* Polarity

with *Nameless, Not Even* Self of *Trans-gnostic Antistential Mind* (☶)

(pointing respectively to these two hexagram in Figure 11).

Next, I Ching's *twenty-second* hexagram.

In Tao of Onliness I Ching it's called

Non-attaining, All-ness Self of *Mind*

(pointing to this hexagram in Figure 11):

(Non-attaining, All-ness Self of *Mind)*

Here is the *image* of this hexagram

(pointing to a photo in his album) (Photo #52),

and Your words are its profound Voice or *text*:

> "Weaver of conception,
>
> embrace your own self-sense mortality.
>
> Know it indifferently
>
> as neither real nor unreal, and both.
>
> Realize *Self* only.
>
> Not just in your mind,
>
> but in your Heart.
>
> Choicelessly, Be Noneother Than."
>
> -Recluse Sage

This, its Tao of Onliness *expression*:

In singular Pan-gnostic Existence;

Mind experience's *power* of *trans-ceptive Boundlessness*

in *fundamental* Polarity with

Mind awareness' *vision* of *holo-ceptive Unconditionality*

Mind compassion's *soul* of *Genesis*

fused in *cardinal* Polarity with

Mind knowledge's *psyche* of *Morphosis*

Mind righteousness' *soul* of *With-ness unreflexivity*

in *elemental* Polarity with

Mind intuition's *psyche* of *Through-ness reflexivity*

Expressed in Prim-istent Reality,

it is *Non-attaining, All-ness* Self of *Trans-gnostic Existential Mind,*

this *Non-attaining, All-ness* Self of Mind reality (☵),

fused in *universive* Polarity

with *Buddha-nature* Self of *Pan-gnostic Antistential Mind* (☰)

(pointing respectively to these two hexagram in Figure 11).

Recluse woman sleeps upon the grass.

Drifter puts his diagram away.

From his pack he takes two oranges,

two peanut butter sandwiches,

a jar of macadamia nuts,

and a thermos of tomato juice.

Recluse wakens, stretches and sits up.

The two share their lunch in silence.

After clean-up drifter takes a nap.

The songs of birds fill the air with sound.

Recluse climbs on rocks among the trees,

now and then stopping to view the sea.

Drifter wakens as recluse returns.

She drinks from the water of the falls,

then lies down on the grass and sleeps.

Drifter too drinks from the waterfall,

then takes out his paper from the pack

and puts it on the ground before him.

Lo: Freely arising from, returning to

supreme Realm's Self of Pan-gnostic Nonbeing Mind (☷)

are these two *universive* Realms of Mind:

First, this *fiftieth* I Ching hexagram.

In Tao of Onliness I Ching it's called

Tao Self of *Mind*

(pointing to this hexagram in Figure 11):

(*Tao* Self of *Mind*)

Here is the *image* of this hexagram

(pointing to a photo in his album) (Photo #53),

and these words are its profound Voice or *text*:

> "Forgetting his oneness with thee (Brahman),
>
> Bewildered by his weakness,

Full of sorrow is man;

But let him look close on thee,

Know thee as himself,

O Lord, most worshipful,

And behold thy glory-

Lo, all his heavy sorrow

Is turned to joy."

-from *The Upanishads*

This, its Tao of Onliness *expression*:

In singular Pan-gnostic Existence;

Mind awareness' trans-symbolic *configurative* Self

Mind knowledge's *Omniscient psyche*

Mind intuition's *scient psyche* of *whole Envisioning*

Expressed in Prim-istent Reality,

it is *Tao* Self *Trans-gnostic Istential Mind.*

This *Tao* Self of Mind reality (☷)

(pointing to this hexagram in Figure 11).

Next, *thirty-second* I Ching hexagram.

In Tao of Onliness I Ching it's called

Absolute Self of *Mind*

(pointing to this hexagram in Figure 11):

(*Absolute* Self of *Mind*)

Here is the *image* of this hexagram
(pointing to a photo in his album) (Photo #54),
and these words are its profound Voice or *text*:

"Do you want to improve the world?
I don't think it can be done.

The world is sacred. It can't be improved.
If you tamper with it, you'll ruin it.
If you treat it like an object, you'll lose it.

There is a time for being ahead, a time for being behind;
a time for being in motion, a time for being at rest;
a time for being vigorous, a time for being exhausted;
a time for being safe, a time for being in danger.

The Master sees things as they are,
without trying to control them.
She lets them go their own way,
and resides at the center of the circle."

-from *Tao Te Ching* (Stephen Mitchell

Translation)

This, its Tao of Onliness *expression*:

In singular Pan-gnostic Existence;

Mind awareness' trans-mental *mind-psyche* of *Reflexivity*

Mind knowledge's *joyful Suffusive psyche*

Mind intuition: *psyche* of *knowledge's Void*

Expressed in Prim-istent Reality,

it is *Absolute* Self of *Pan-gnostic Istential Mind.*

This *Absolute* Self of Mind Reality (☰)

(pointing to this hexagram in Figure 11).

Recluse woman opens up her eyes.

Drifter's eyes gaze across the land,

then look out on the shimmering sea.

He turns and looks down at the pool.

Undulating on its surface

is the fluid shadow of his head.

He stares at this dancing silhouette

floating on the face of the water.

Recluse sits up and looks about.

Drifter views his fluid silhouette.

Lo: This undulating shadow silhouette (pointing)

is my egoic self reality.

This is the self of my identity.

This focused and fascinating shadow

is but a phantom of transcendent Self

projected on a lesser dimension

of Absolute Dimensionality.

Merely a shade of Self reality.

I Am the seamless *Truth* of Onliness.

These are the Yin-Yang *Paths* which I Follow.

Sage, *This* is *My Way of* Enlightenment;

also, It is the *Way* through which *I Teach*.

But I still have a long, long way to go.

Both sit in silence for awhile.

Drifter views his watery shadow.

Recluse looks upon the distant sea.

Drifter returns to his diagram.

Lo: Again emerging from, returning to

supreme Realm's Self of Trans-gnostic Being Mind (☷)

are these two *universive* Realms of Mind:

First, this *sixty-third* I Ching hexagram.

In Tao of Onliness I Ching it's called

Undivided Self of *Mind*

(pointing to this hexagram in Figure 11):

⚏⚎ (hexagram figure)

(*Undivided* Self of *Mind*)

Here is the *image* of this hexagram

(pointing to a photo in his album) (Photo #55),

and Your words are its profound Voice or *text*:

> "Vagabond drifter,
>
> be not deluded by mind duality;
>
> this attachment to conception and desire.
>
> This prison of your own self-imposition.
>
>
> Every moment Here is Bliss,
>
> every moment Freedom.
>
> Beloved, *all* of It is Thou.
>
> —Recluse Sage

This, its Tao of Onliness *expression*:

In singular Pan-gnostic Existence;

Mind experience's trans-symbolic *transfigurative* Self

in *fundamental* Polarity with

Mind awareness' trans-symbolic *configurative* Self

Mind compassion's *Omnipotent soul*

fused in *cardinal* Polarity with

Mind knowledge's *Omniscient psyche*

Mind righteousness' *lucent soul* of *dispassionate Passion*

in *elemental* Polarity with

Mind intuition's *scient psyche* of *whole Envisioning*

Expressed in Prim-istent Reality,

it is *Undivided* Self of *Pan-gnostic Transexistential Mind,*

this *Undivided* Self of Mind Reality (☷),

fused in *universive* Polarity

with *Tao* Self of *Trans-gnostic Istential Mind* (☶)

(pointing respectively to these two hexagram in Figure 11).

Next, *thirty-seventh* I Ching hexagram.

In Tao of Onliness I Ching it's called

Non-clinging, Non-attachment Self of *Mind*

(pointing to this hexagram in Figure 11):

(*Non-clinging, Non-attachment* Self of *Mind*)

Here is the *image* of this hexagram

(pointing to a photo in his album) (Photo #56),

and Your words are its profound Voice or *text*:

"Slayer of phantoms, see this ripple on the stream?

This is your space-time mind-body *self* of consciousness.

This whole/part holonic ego self.

Just like this ripple of the stream,

the mind-body *self* appears, evolves and disappears.

But the Water of Consciousness of which this ripple is,

is Seamless, Boundless, and Unconditional,

even as It Manifests *this* way of rippling.

Awakening gypsy, *You* are this ripple apparency

and the birthless, deathless Water of the Stream."

-Recluse Sage

This, its Tao of Onliness *expression*:

In singular Pan-gnostic Existence;

Mind experience's trans-mental *heart-soul* of *Unreflexivity*

in *fundamental* Polarity with

Mind awareness' trans-mental *mind-psyche* of *Reflexivity*

Mind compassion's *intense Infusive soul*

fused in *cardinal* Polarity with

Mind knowledge's *joyful Suffusive psyche*

Mind righteousness: *soul* of *compassion's Void*

in *elemental* Polarity with

Mind intuition: *psyche* of *knowledge's Void*

Expressed in Prim-istent Reality,

it is *Non-clinging, Non-attachment* Self of *Trans-gnostic Transexistential Mind*,

this *Non-clinging, Non-attachment* Self of Mind Reality ($\equiv\!\equiv$), fused in *universe* Polarity

with *Absolute* Self of *Pan-gnostic Istential Mind* (☷)

(pointing respectively to these two hexagrams in Figure 11).

Recluse lies back viewing the blue sky

and scattered clouds floating overhead.

Mid has turned to late afternoon.

Drifter looks up at the waterfall

and listens to its splashing song.

Recluse woman rises to her feet.

Drifter gets up and puts on his pack.

Recluse leads the way up steep inclines

through the trees and into the clearing,

climbing 'til they reach the mountain top.

Here they are surrounded by the sea.

Two silent isolated figures

standing on the windswept mountain top

viewing the blue ocean's majesty.

All around them are the distant shores

of this emerald tropic island.

Windblown, they stand facing Northward,

looking out upon the vast ocean.

Recluse: Island, sea, and crystal dreams,

        which is the seer and which the seen?

Flickering light of shadow streams,

which is the seemer and which the seemed?

Eye of Onliness vagabond,

I Am *beyond* duality, *beyond* boundary, *beyond* conditionality.

I Am Enlightenment *with no second.*

Visionary word carpenter,

I Am.

Beloved, You and I are *One* Destiny!

We are seamless Eternity!

A monarch butterfly hovers,

then alights upon drifter's shoulder.

Recluse woman turns and touches it.

The butterfly explodes in flame.

In a horrendous fiery burst

engulfing this whole reality,

man, woman, mountain, island, sea, sky -

all of this reality consumed.

The flame alone is and remains.

Slowly it too fades and is no more.

Beyond Arch-istential Consciousness,

This Realm, only Unmanifest, of

transpolar Trans-consciousness *Omnists.*

This Omni-transholist Consciousness.

Omnistent Omni-transholist Self.

Unfathomable, unknowable,

Trans-holistent Omnisting "remains."

CHAPTER TEN

The Flower of Prim-holistent Onliness

X

"*Entering the City with Bliss-bestowing Hands.* His thatched cottage gate is closed, and even the wisest know him not. No glimpses of his inner life are to be caught; for he goes on his own way without following the steps of the ancient sages. Carrying a gourd he goes out into the market, leaning against a staff he comes home. He is found in company with wine-bibbers and butchers, he and they are all converted into Buddhas.

Bare-chested and bare-footed, he comes out into the
    market-place;
Daubed with mud and ashes, how broadly he smiles!
There is no need for the miraculous power of the gods,
For he touches, and lo! the dead trees are in full
    bloom."

-from "The Ten Oxherding Pictures"
by Kaku-an
-compiled by D. T. Suzuki
from *Manual of Zen Buddhism*

"Going *within* and *beyond* even this pure Source and pure Spirit [Causal]—which is totally formless, boundless, unmanifest—the Self/Spirit awakens to an identity with, and as, *all* Form, . . . whether high or low, ascending or descending, sacred or profane, manifest or unmanifest, finite or infinite, temporal or eternal. This [Non-dual Ground] is not a particular stage among other stages— not their Goal, not their Source, not their Summit—but rather the Ground or Suchness or Isness of *all* stages, at all times, in all dimensions . . . When one breaks through the causal absorption in pure unmanifest and unborn Spirit, the entire manifest world (or worlds) arises once again, but this time as a perfect expression of Spirit and as Spirit. The Formless and the entire world of manifest Form . . . are seen to be not-two (or nondual)."

-Ken Wilber
from *Sex, Ecology, Spirituality:*
The Spirit of Evolution
(see Appendix C)

"Listen to the wind among the pines (pointing to the pine trees above them).

It whispers one Word only - 'Consciousness.' "

"Fish-catcher of visionary dreams,

I Am *Self* - boundless, birthless, deathless.

No-thing at All.

I Am Enlightenment *with no second*.

Fish-fryer of luminous schemes,

I Am.

Beloved, You and I are *One* Destiny!

We *are* Consciousness, Wind among the Pines!"

A dry wind is gusting through the trees.

Learned one turns round and looks at mute.

Mute is looking skyward at the pines.

Drifter too looks at the swaying pines.

On a ridge high up the mountain side

these two walk in shade of the pine trees.

Below them lies a vast desert floor

of giant rocks, sage, and dry grasses.

Above them, the rocky mountain top.

Lo: Sage, thank you for these Words You share with me.

 I See the *Self* of My own mountain top.

 Not attained, but That which I ever Am.

 But I still mediate with conception,

 still cling to my ego identity.

 But for me now there is *no* turning back.

 I Realize that *I Am* Consciousness

 and have no longer any place to hide.

 Through meditative Paths of Onliness

 I glimpse *directly* My true Destiny;

 See that I Am *only* Enlightenment.

Leaving the wooded ridge behind,

they ascend a long grassy incline

which leads them toward the mountain top.

Mute and drifter continue to climb

up steep ravines, along rock ledges,

until they reach the rocky summit.

They stand on this peak and look about.

Arid desert stretches before them

with large mountains scattered round about.

They stand in a cool, gusting wind

viewing this majestic desert scene.

In a rock-bound shelter near the peak

mute and drifter sit down facing North.

In the shade of this rocky cove,

mute takes out, fills, and lights his pipe.

Drifter views the distant desert floor.

Scent of sage and pine float on the air.

Morning has nearly turned to noon.

Sagebrush and scrub trees surround the cove.

Seated in silent contemplation,

both look out upon this desert view.

Black hawks circle slowly high above.

Mute lies back upon a tuft of grass

and watches as they glide overhead.

Drifter moves to face the cove's rock wall

and sits zazen in meditation.

Soon Mute too sits zazen with drifter.

Noon turns to early afternoon.

Mute takes a canteen from drifter's pack.

They drink deeply from this water source.

Drifter then removes two diagrams

and puts these before them on the ground.

Lo: This *Tao of Onliness* Polarity (gesturing to Figure 12).

     Flower of Prim-holistent Onliness (continuing to gesture to Figure 12)

     from Point of View of Onliness Itself

     as Seen through Pan-gnostic Existent eyes.

     I speak of Tao of Onliness I Ching

     and of Its Onliness Polarity

     (pointing to the fourth-ring Yin and Yang Onliness quadrigrams of

     Figure 4).

     These *absolute* Onliness Realms are called

     Self of *Yang Onliness* Enlightenment (☱)

     and *Self* of *Yin Onliness* Enlightenment (☳),

     here fused in *absolute* Polarity

     (pointing respectively to these two innermost quadrigrams of Figure 12).

Putting the large diagram away (Figure 4),

drifter takes out his photo album.

Mute lies with his hands behind his head

looking up at a clear blue sky.

Sage around them rustle in the wind.

Drifter views the distant dry valley

bathed in sunlight of the afternoon.

Figure 12

Mute closes his eyes and falls asleep.

Drifter looks down at his diagram.

Lo: Freely emerging from, returning to

Self of Yang Onliness Enlightenment's *absolute* Reality (⚎)

(pointing to this quadrigram in Figure 12)

are these two *supreme* Realms of Onliness:

Self of Trans-gnostic Nonbeing Onliness (☳)

and Self of Pan-gnostic Nonbeing Onliness (☶)

(pointing respectively to these two pentagrams in Figure 12).

Likewise arising from, returning to

Self of Yin Onliness Enlightenment's *absolute* Reality (⚍)

(pointing to this quadrigram in Figure 12)

are these two *supreme* Realms of Onliness:

Self of Pan-gnostic Being Onliness (☴)

in greater *supreme* Polarity with

Self of Trans-gnostic Nonbeing Onliness (☳)

(pointing respectively to these two pentagrams in Figure 12),

and Self of Trans-gnostic Being Onliness (☴)

in lesser *supreme* Polarity with

Self of Pan-gnostic Nonbeing Onliness (☶)

(pointing respectively to these two pentagrams in Figure 12).

Drifter looks upon the great beauty

of the arid wilderness below.

Mute's eyes open. He slowly sits up

and views the distant mountain range.

Both drifter and mute slowly stand up.

Mute walks from the shelter of the cove.

Some distance away he urinates.

Mute and drifter both walk from the cove

and circle the crescent of the peak.

Sagebrush and parched grass grow here and there.

Wild flowers bloom between the rocks.

They stop and stand on a windy ledge

and view the great mountains near to them,

dry and barren in the summer sun.

Mute and drifter reach the mountain's peak

and climb on the highest boulder there.

Turning slowly in the gusting winds,

drifter views this panoramic scene.

A rugged and desolate landscape

as far as drifter's eyes can see.

Mute twirls round and begins to dance.

A blend of tap dance and Irish Jig,

marking rhythm with his hands and feet.

A spritely dance there upon the rock,

his beard and hair blowing in the wind.

Learned one watches with amusement,

and soon he too joins the mute in dance.

With abandon, swirling round about,

laughing and howling as they dance.

Finally they both fall to the ground.

Lying there, they look up at the sky.

After a time they climb off the rock

and walk down to their sheltered cove.

Mute sits down, then fills and lights his pipe.

Drifter gets his paper from the pack,

sits down and spreads it upon the ground.

Lo: Arising from and thence returning to

supreme Realm's Self of Pan-gnostic Nonbeing Onliness (☷)

are two *universive* Onliness Realms:

First, this *fifty-fifth* I Ching hexagram.

In Tao of Onliness I Ching it's called

Uncreated Self of *Onliness*

(pointing to this hexagram in Figure 12):

(*Uncreated* Self of *Onliness*)

This is the *image* of this hexagram

(pointing to a photo in his album) (Photo #57),

and these words are its profound Voice or *text*:

> "The kingdom of God cometh not with observation:
>
> Neither shall they say,
>
> Lo here! or, lo there!
>
> for, behold, the kingdom of God is within you."
>
> -Jesus
>
> from *The Holy Bible* (Luke 17:20-21)

This, its Tao of Onliness *expression*:

In singular Pan-gnostic Existence;

Onliness experience's *omnipotent* Consciousness

Onliness compassion's *germinating Form of emptiness*

Onliness righteousness' *soul: searing fire* of Worlds

Expressed in Prim-istent Reality,

it is *Uncreated* Self of *Pan-gnostic Istential Onliness.*

This *Uncreated* Self of Onliness Reality (☵)

(pointing to this hexagram in Figure 12).

Second, I Ching's *thirtieth* hexagram.

In Tao of Onliness I Ching it's called

No-separation, Oneness Self of *Onliness*

(pointing to this hexagram in Figure 12):

(*No-separation, Oneness* Self of *Onliness*)

Here is the *image* of this hexagram

(pointing to a photo in his album) (Photo #58),

and these words are its profound Voice or *text*:

"Notice conditional forms and events and activities

as they arise or continue or change or pass away,

but Simply and Constantly and Merely Be and Recognize

Your Self As The Self-Radiant Consciousness or Self-Existing Love-Bliss

In, Of, and As Whom all conditional forms, events, and activities

Are presently arising, continuing, changing, or passing away.

Notice conditional forms, events, and activities,

but Notice (and Thus Inherently Transcend) them In, Of, and As

Your Very Self, Which Is Transcendental and Infinitely Expanded,

Beyond and Prior To all conditions."

-Da Free John

from *The Dawn Horse Testament*

This, its Tao of Onliness *expression*:

In singular Pan-gnostic Existence;

Onliness experience's *genesis* of *Creativity*

Onliness compassion's *soul* of *Sight*

Onliness righteousness' *soul* of *each each-where Enfoldingness*

Expressed in Prim-istent Reality,

it is *No-separation, Oneness* Self of *Trans-gnostic Istential Onliness*.

This *No-separation, Oneness* Self of Onliness Reality (☷)

(pointing to this hexagram in Figure 12).

Mute looks out upon this desert land.

Learned one sits with his eyes closed.

His eyes open to a small cactus

growing in a crack between two rocks

and flowering in its full red bloom.

He looks at this flower a long time.

Meanwhile, mute stands up and stretches,

then explores the rocky shelf they're on.

He returns and sits down by drifter.

Drifter views his flower diagram.

Lo: Sage, emerging from and returning to

supreme Realm's Self of Trans-gnostic Being Onliness (☷)

are two *universive* Onliness Realms:

First, I Ching's *fifty-seventh* hexagram.

In Tao of Onliness I Ching it's called

Timeless Self of *Onliness*

(pointing to this hexagram in Figure 12):

(*Timeless* Self of *Onliness*)

Here is the *image* of this hexagram

(pointing to a photo in his album) (Photo #59),

and these words are its profound Voice of *text*:

"Shuzan (Shou-shan, 926-992) once held up his *shippe*

(a short stick made with split bamboo and bound with ratan)

to an assembly of his disciples and declared:

'Call this a *shippe* and you assert;

call it not a *shippe* and you negate.

Now, do not assert nor negate, and what would you call it?

Speak, speak!'

One of the disciples came out of the ranks,

took the *shippe* away from the master,

and breaking it in two, exclaimed 'What is this?'"

-from *An Introduction to Zen Buddhism*

by D. T. Suzuki

This, its Tao of Onliness *expression*:

In singular Pan-gnostic Existence;

Onliness awareness' *omniscient* Consciousness

in *fundamental* Polarity with

Onliness experience's *omnipotent* Consciousness

Onliness knowledge's *flowering Void of formlessness*

fused in *cardinal* Polarity with

Onliness compassion's *germinating Form of emptiness*

Onliness intuition's *psyche: creator* and *destroyer* of Worlds

in *elemental* Polarity with

Onliness righteousness' *soul: searing fire* of Worlds

Expressed in Prim-istent Reality,

it is *Timeless* Self of *Trans-gnostic Transexistential Onliness*,

this *Timeless* Self of Onliness Reality (☰),

fused in *universive* Polarity

with *Uncreated* Self of *Pan-gnostic Istential Onliness* (☷)

(pointing respectively to these two hexagrams in Figure 12).

Second, I Ching's *forty-eighth* hexagram.

In Tao of Onliness I Ching it's called

Unfathomable Self of *Onliness*

(pointing to this hexagram in Figure 12):

(*Unfathomable* Self of *Onliness*)

This is the *image* of this hexagram
(pointing to a photo in his album) (Photo #60),
and these words are its profound Voice or *text*:

> "The Master keeps her mind
> always at one with the Tao;
> that is what gives her her radiance.
>
> The Tao is ungraspable.
> How can her mind be at one with it?
> Because she doesn't cling to ideas.
>
> The Tao is dark and unfathomable.
> How can it make her radiant?
> Because she lets it.
>
> Since before time and space were, the Tao is.
> It is beyond *is* and *is not*.
> How do I know this is true?
> I look inside myself and see."

-Lao-tzu (from *Tao Te Ching*)

Stephen Mitchell Translation

This, its Tao of Onliness *expression*:

In singular Pan-gnostic Existence;

Onliness awareness' *morphosis* of *Productivity*

in *fundamental* Polarity with

Onliness experience's *genesis* of *Creativity*

Onliness knowledge's *psyche* of *Insight*

fused in *cardinal* Polarity with

Onliness compassion's *soul* of *Sight*

Onliness intuition's *psyche* of *all all-where Boundlessness*

in *elemental* Polarity with

Onliness righteousness' *soul* of *each each-where Enfoldingness*

Expressed in Prim-istent Reality,

it is *Unfathomable* Self of *Pan-gnostic Transexistential Onliness*,

this *Unfathomable* Self of Onliness Reality (☷),

fused in *universive* Polarity

with the *No-separation, Oneness* Self of *Trans-gnostic Istential Onliness* (☶)

(pointing respectively to these two hexagrams in Figure 12).

Early has turned to mid afternoon.

Mute lies asleep upon the ground.

Drifter looks out on desert vistas.

From his backpack learned one removes

cod filet on hardroll sandwiches,

can of almonds and jar of grape juice,

two carrots, and two large oranges.

Mute soon awakens and sits up.

The two share this late lunch in silence.

Learned one lies back and takes a nap.

Mute cleans up, then walks about the ledge.

He stops at the ravine's precipice

bordering their sheltered rocky cove.

Mute stands gazing into this abyss.

He returns, lies down and takes a nap.

Crows circle and call out overhead.

A warm dry breeze rustles through the sage.

Mute and drifter sleep in desert bliss

on this mountain ledge in the cove's shade.

Learned one awakens and sits up

just as a chipmunk scurries by.

Taking his paper from the pack,

he unfolds it upon the ground.

Lo: Freely arising from, returning to

    supreme Realm's Self of Trans-gnostic Nonbeing Onliness (☰̲)

    are two *universive* Onliness Realms:

    First, this *forty-ninth* I Ching hexagram.

    In Tao of Onliness I Ching it's called

Unspeakable Self of *Onliness*

(pointing to this hexagram in Figure 12):

(*Unspeakable* Self of *Onliness*)

Here is the *image* of this hexagram

(pointing to a photo in his album) (Photo #61),

and these words are its profound Voice or *text*:

> "From the first not a thing is."
>
> -Hui-neng
>
> from *The Zen Doctrine of No-Mind*
>
> by D. T. Suzuki

This, its Tao of Onliness *expression*:

In singular Pan-gnostic Existence;

Onliness experience's *Unconditional Gnostic heart-soul*

Onliness compassion's *soul* of *Grace*

Onliness righteousness' *apprehending power* of *Love*

Expressed in Prim-istent Reality,

it is *Unspeakable* Self of *Pan-gnostic Antistential Onliness*.

This *Unspeakable* Self of Onliness Reality (☷)

(pointing to this hexagram in Figure 12).

Second, this *thirteenth* I Ching hexagram.

In Tao of Onliness I Ching it's called

Ultimate Self of *Onliness*

(pointing to this hexagram in Figure 12):

(*Ultimate* Self of *Onliness*)

Here is the *image* or this hexagram

(pointing to a photo in his album) (Photo #62),

and these words are its profound Voice or *text*:

> "Whoever knows himself knows God. . .
>
> Wherever you turn is God's face."
>
> -Muhammad
>
> from *The Enlightened Mind*
>
> compiled by Stephen Mitchell

This, its Tao of Onliness *expression*:

In singular Pan-gnostic Existence;

Onliness experience's Numinous *apparent transparency*

Onliness compassion's trans-symbolic *Conceptive soul*

Onliness righteousness' *soul* of *Vitality*

Expressed in Prim-istent Reality,

it is *Ultimate* Self of *Trans-gnostic Antistential Onliness*.

This *Ultimate* Self of Onliness Reality (☰)

(pointing to this hexagram in Figure 12).

Mute stirs, opens his eyes and sits up.

Drifter looks out on this vast expanse.

A song bird's warble breaks the silence.

Leaves rustle in nearby scrub trees.

Lo: Sage, I Am *Self* of No-separation;

    no self-imposed division boundaries.

    No *thing* to strive for and no *thing* to gain.

    Subject-object duality recedes.

    In this way "I" of ego fades away.

    Non-dual Self of *Truth* thus Manifests.

Drifter looks out across the valley

staring at the mountains to the North.

Mute closes his eyes in deep repose.

For a long time they so meditate.

Drifter looks down at his diagram.

Lo: Likewise arising from, returning to

    supreme Realm's Self of Pan-gnostic Being Onliness (☷)

    are two *universive* Onliness Realms:

First, this *eighteenth* hexagram of I Ching.

In Tao of Onliness I Ching it's called

All-present, No-ness Self of *Onliness*

(pointing to this hexagram in Figure 12):

(*All-present, No-ness* Self of *Onliness*)

Here is the *image* of this hexagram

(pointing to a photo in his album) (Photo #63),

and these words are its profound Voice or *text*:

> "Bodhi (Knowledge of the Buddha-Nature) is no state.
>
> The Buddha did not attain to it.
>
> Sentient beings do not lack it.
>
> It cannot be reached with the body
>
> nor sought with the mind.
>
> All sentient beings are already of one form with Bodhi."
>
> -Huang Po
>
> quoted from *Eye To Eye*
>
> by Ken Wilber

This, its Tao of Onliness *expression*:

In singular Pan-gnostic Existence;

Onliness awareness' *boundless Gnostic mind-psyche*

in *fundamental* Polarity with

Onliness experience's *unconditional Gnostic heart-soul*

Onliness knowledge's *psyche* of *Essence*

fused in *cardinal* Polarity with

Onliness compassion's *soul* of *Grace*

Onliness intuition's *comprehending harvest* of *Insight*

in *elemental* Polarity with

Onliness righteousness' *apprehending power* of *Love*

Expressed in Prim-istent Reality,

it is *All-present, No-ness* Self of *Trans-gnostic Existential Onliness*,

this *All-present, No-ness* Self of Onliness Reality (☷),

fused in *universive* Polarity

with *Unspeakable* Self of *Pan-gnostic Antistential Onliness* (☷)

(pointing respectively to these two hexagrams in Figure 12).

Second, *forty-sixth* I Ching hexagram.

In Tao of Onliness I Ching it's called

Supreme Self of *Onliness*

(pointing to this hexagram in Figure 12):

(*Supreme* Self of *Onliness*)

This is the *image* of this hexagram
(pointing to a photo in his album) (Photo #64),
and these words are its profound Voice or *text*:

"The eye through which I see God
is the same eye through which God sees me;
my eye and God's eye are one eye,
one seeing, one knowing, one love."

- Meister Eckhart

quoted from *The Enlightened Mind*

compiled by Stephen Mitchell

This, its Tao of Onliness *expression*:
In singular Pan-gnostic Existence;
Onliness awareness' Numinous *transparent apparency*
in *fundamental* Polarity with
Onliness experience's Numinous *apparent transparency*
Onliness knowledge's trans-symbolic *Prehending psyche*
fused in *cardinal* Polarity with
Onliness compassion's trans-symbolic *Conceptive soul*
Onliness intuition's *psyche* of *Trans-ideation*
in *elemental* Polarity with

Onliness righteousness' *soul* of *Vitality*

Expressed in Prim-istent Reality,

it is *Supreme* Self of *Pan-gnostic Existential Onliness*,

this *Supreme* Self of Onliness Reality (☲),

fused in *universive* Polarity

with *Ultimate* Self of *Trans-gnostic Antistential Onliness* (☳)

(pointing respectively to these two hexagrams in Figure 12).

Learned one looks at the cactus-bloom.

Mute looks on this panoramic view.

A gust of wind stirs along the ledge.

Mute stretches, then rises to his feet.

Slowly he walks to the precipice.

Drifter intently watches him.

He then joins mute at the precipice.

From his pocket mute removes his pipe,

tossing it into the deep ravine.

It falls through the air two hundred feet.

Where it shatters on the rocks below,

this reality bursts into flame.

A massive fiery explosion

engulfs this whole reality;

mute, drifter, cove, mountain, desert, sky -

all of this reality consumed.

The flame alone is and remains.

Slowly it too fades and is no more.

Transcending Omnistent Consciousness,

Trans-manifest and Trans-istential,

Consciousness with no second Trans-ists -

Only Self of Enlightenment.

Unfathomable, unknowable,

boundless Self of Consciousness "remains."

Appendix A
Page Location of Each I Ching Hexagram:

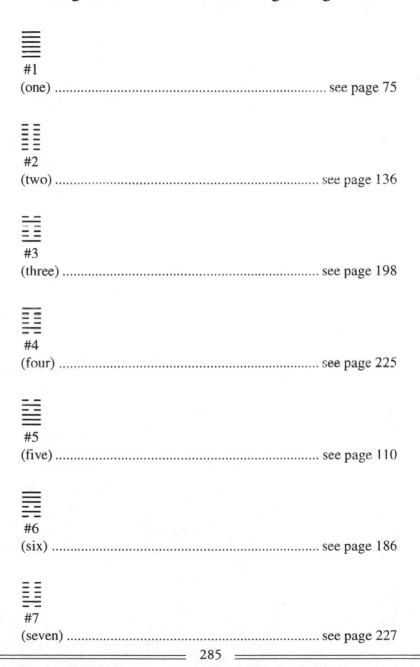

#1
(one) .... see page 75

#2
(two) .... see page 136

#3
(three) .... see page 198

#4
(four) .... see page 225

#5
(five) .... see page 110

#6
(six) .... see page 186

#7
(seven) .... see page 227

☷☵

#8

☴☰

#9

☰☱

#10

☷☰

#11

☰☷

#12

☰☲

#13

☲☰

#14

☷☶

#15

≣≣

#16

☰☰

#17

☲☲

#18

☳☳

#19

☶☶

#20

☲☲

#21

☶☶

#22

☶☶

#23

☷☳
#24

☰☳
#25

☰☶
#26

☶☳
#27

☱☴
#28

☵☵
#29

☲☲
#30

☱☶
#31

☷☵
#48

☱☵
#49

☲☷
#50

☳☳
#51

☶☷
#52

☴☶
#53

☳☱
#54

☳☲
#55

☷

#64

Appendix B
Tao of Onliness I Ching Line Designations:

sample I Ching hexagrams:

6th line: *universive* line of Prim-istence

5th line: *supreme* line of Prim-istence

4th line: *absolute* line of Prim-istence

3rd line: *elemental* line of singular Pan-gnostic Existence

2nd line: *cardinal* line of singular Pan-gnostic Existence

1st line: *fundamental* line of singular Pan-gnostic Existence

Appendix C

This modified Figure 2 graph describes the relation and correspondence between (1) the Tao of Onliness cosmology's transcendental (transpersonal) levels and evolutionary/developmental stages of Consciousness or Reality (Self), and (2) the transcendental (transpersonal) evolutionary/developmental stages of Consciousness described by Ken Wilber (1995) and others i.e., Psychic, Subtle, and Causal Stages, and Nondual Ground. Note that both cosmologies are holonic in nature i.e., each holon is a whole/part that includes but transcends (negates but preserves) each and every lower level. This is the meaning of the arrows at the upper border of the page pointing so as to include (but transcend) all lower levels. The arrow of Nondual Ground (Wilber) or Consciousness/Self (Treon) at the lower border of the page points to unconditional and boundless Consciousness or Self.

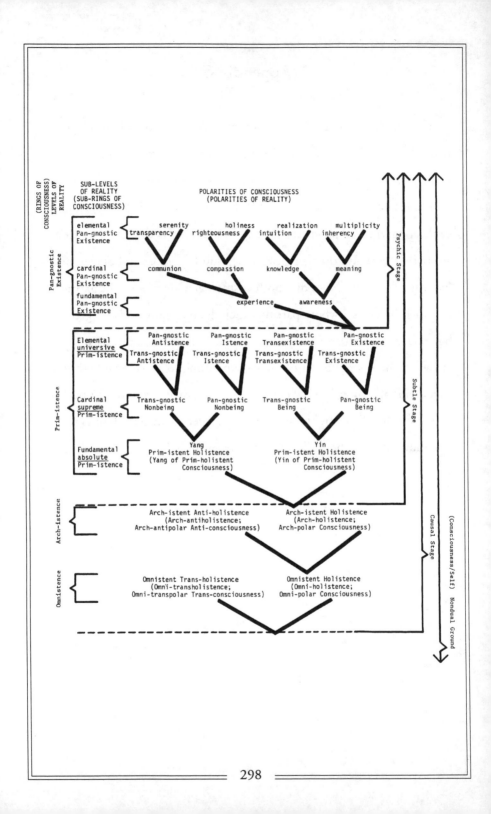

Appendix D
Reference to often Cited Figures 2A, 3, and 4

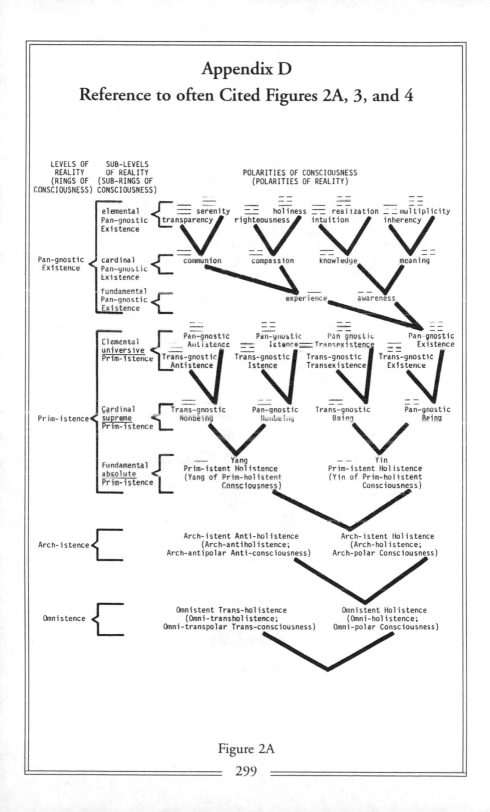

Figure 2A

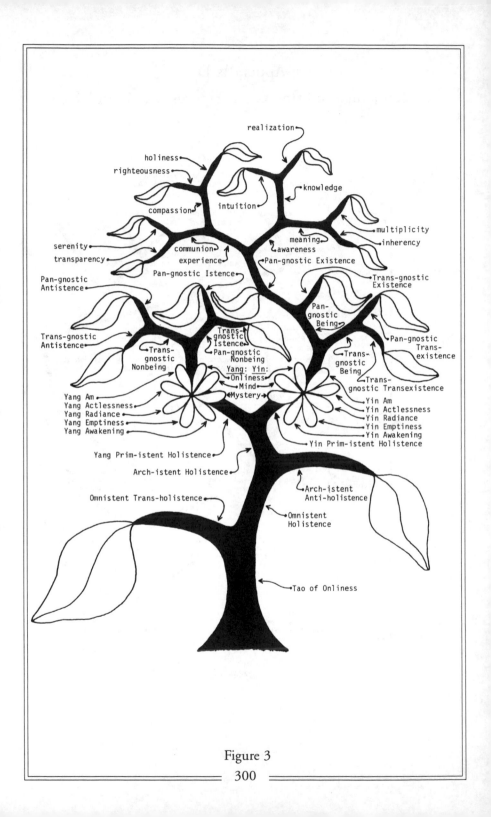

Figure 3

Figure 4

References

Blofeld, J. (translator and editor) (1968). *I Ching: The Book of Change*. New York: E. P. Dutton and Co.

Castaneda, C. (1984). *The Fire From Within*. New York: Simon and Schuster, Inc.

Da Free John (1985). *The Dawn Horse Testament of Heart-Master Da Free John*. San Rafael, CA: The Dawn Horse Press.

The Holy Bible (King James Version). New York: World Publishing Co.

The Jerusalem Bible (1968). Garden City, NY: Doubleday and Co.

Kapleau, Philip (compiler) (1965). *The Three Pillars of Zen: Teaching Practice Enlightenment*. Boston: Beacon Press.

Legge, J. (translator and editor) (1964). *I Ching: Book of Changes*. New York: Bantam Books, Inc.

McNaughton, W. (translator) (1971). *The Taoist Vision*. Ann Arbor, MI: University of Michigan Press.

Merrell-Wolff, F. (1973). *Pathways Through To Space: A Personal Record of Transformation in Consciousness*. New York: Warner Books, Inc.

Meyer, M. W. (translator) (1984). *The Secret Teaching of Jesus: Four Gnostic Gospels*. New York: Vintage Books (Random House).

Mitchell, Stephen (compiler) (1992). *The Enlightened Heart: An Anthology of Poetry*. New York: Harper.

Mitchell, Stephen (compiler) (1991). *The Enlightened Mind: An Anthology of Sacred Prose*. New York: Harper.

Mitchell, Stephen (translator) (1991). *Tao Te Ching: A New English Version*. New York: HarperCollins Publishers.

Reps, P. (compiler) (1957). *Zen Flesh, Zen Bones: A Collection of Zen and Pre-Zen Writings*. Tokyo and Rutland, VT: Charles E. Tuttle Co.

Suzuki, D. T. (1972). *The Zen Doctrine of No-Mind.* York Beach, MA: Samuel Weiser.

Suzuki, D. T. (1964). *An Introduction to Zen Buddhism.* New York: Grove Press.

Suzuki, D. T. (compiler) (1960). *Manual of Zen Buddhism.* New York: Grove Press, Inc.

Swami Prabhavananda and C. Isherwood (translators) (1960). *The Song of God: Bhagavad-Gita.* New York: Mentor Books (The New American Library).

Swami Prabhavananda and F. Manchester (translators) (1957). *The Upanishads: Breath of the Eternal.* New York: Mentor Books (The New American Library).

Treon, M. (1989). *The Tao of Onliness: An I Ching Cosmology - The Awakening Years.* Santa Barbara, CA: Fithian Press.

Wilber, K. (1995). *Sex, Ecology, Spirituality: The Spirit of Evolution.* Boston: Shambhala Publications, Inc.

Wilber, K. (1990). *Eye to Eye: The Quest for the New Paradigm* (Expanded Edition). Boston: Shambhala Publications, Inc.

Wilber, K. (1981). *Up From Eden: A Transpersonal View of Human Evolution.* New York: Doubleday/Anchor.

Photographic Images Section:
Photographic Images of the Sixty-Four
I Ching Hexagrams

Photo #1 ☰ Numinous Revelation
Self of Am   (see page 75)

Photo #2 ䷫ Infinite Uncontracted
Self of Am   (see page 77)

Photo #3 ䷖
15

Unqualifiable
Self of Am

(see page 80)

Photo #4 ䷳
52

Unsurpassable Transfinite
Self of Am

(see page 82)

Photo #5   ䷔
14

All-embracing
Only Self of Am   (see page 85)

Photo #6   ䷡
34

No-otherness Trans-istential
Self of Am   (see page 87)

Photo #7 ䷦ 39 Non-striving, Non-resisting Self of Am (see page 89)

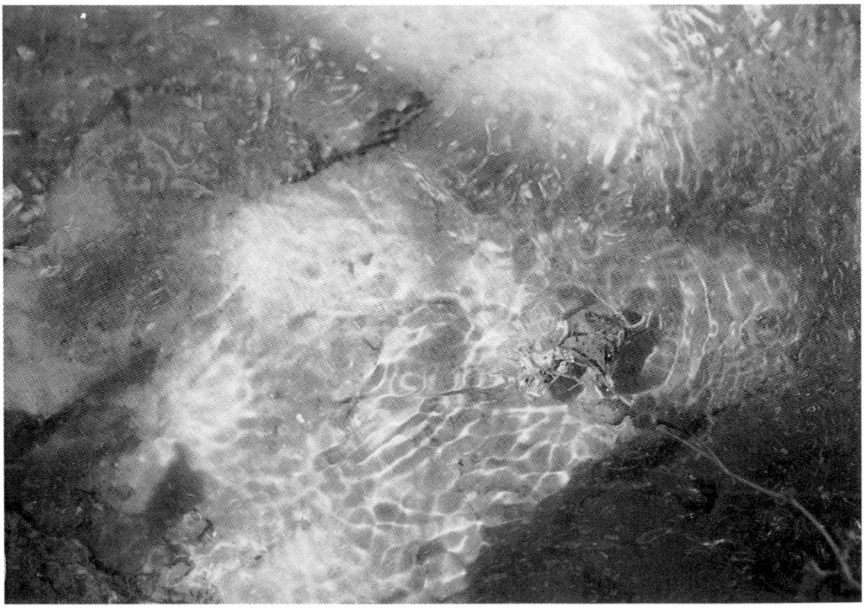

Photo #8 ䷴ 53 Luminous Recognition Self of Am (see page 91)

Photo #9

⚋⚋
⚊⚊
⚋⚋
62

Non-discriminating
Self of Actlessness

(see page 104)

Photo #10 ䷞
56

Changeless
Self of Actlessness

(see page 106)

Photo #11 ䷌
9

God-realized
Self of Actlessness

(see page 108)

Photo #12 No-thingness, No-mind
Self of Actlessness (see page 110)
5

Photo #13 Trans-egoic Meritless
Self of Actlessness (see page 113)
31

Photo #14 ䷝
33

Inherent, Illuminated
Self of Actlessness

(see page 114)

Photo #15 ䷖
26

Unconditional
Self of Actlessness

(see page 118)

Photo #16 ䷊ 11   Unutterable Transcendental
Self of Actlessness   (see page 120)

Photo #17 ䷉ 10   All-inclusive
Self of Radiance   (see page 132)

Photo #18 ䷼
58

Compassionate Omniscient

Self of Radiance   (see page 133)

Photo #19 ䷁
2

Eternal

Self of Radiance   (see page 136)

Photo #20 ䷖
23

Choiceless

Self of Radiance

(see page 138)

Photo #21 ䷨
38

Brahman-consciousness (Atman)

Self of Radiance

(see page 141)

Photo #22   Suchness
54   Self of Radiance   (see page 142)

Photo #23   Christ-consciousness
8   Self of Radiance   (see page 145)

Photo #24 ䷓
20

Seamless
Self of Radiance

(see page 147)

Photo #25 ䷇
16

Formless
Self of Emptiness

(see page 159)

Photo #26 ䷢
35

Boundless
Self of Emptiness

(see page 160)

Photo #27 ䷼
61

Divine
Self of Emptiness

(see page 163)

Photo #28 ䷗
60

Reality
Self of Emptiness

(see page 165)

Photo #29 ䷓
45

Unmediated
Self of Emptiness

(see page 168)

Photo #30 ䷗
12

Ineffable Void
Self of Emptiness

(see page 169)

Photo #31 ䷨ 41

Preferenceless
Self of Emptiness

(see page 172)

Photo #32 ䷖
19

Enlightened
Self of Emptiness

(see page 174)

Photo #33 ䷗
6

All-pervading
Self of Awakening

(see page 186)

Photo #34

47

Compassion (Sacred)
Self of Awakening

(see page 187)

Photo #35 ䷚
24

Trans-manifest
Self of Awakening   (see page 190)

Photo #36 ䷓
27

Omnipresent
Self of Awakening   (see page 192)

Photo #37 ䷿ 64 Innate-nature
Self of Awakening (see page 195)

Photo #38 ䷧ 40 Non-abiding
Self of Awakening (see page 196)

Photo #39 ䷂
3

Birthless, Deathless
Self of Awakening

(see page 198)

Photo #40 ䷜
42

Wisdom (Truth)
Self of Awakening

(see page 200)

Photo #41 ䷲
51

Consciousness
Self of Mystery

(see page 213)

Photo #42 ䷚
21

Alpha and Omega
Self of Mystery

(see page 214)

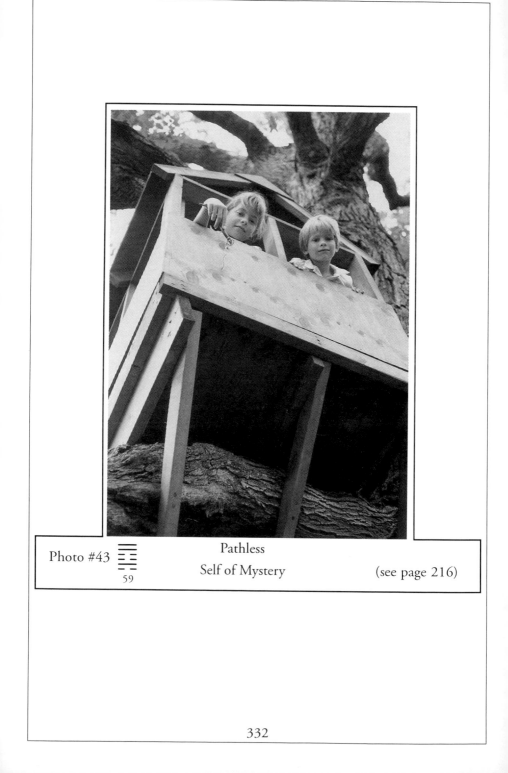

Photo #43 ䷜
59

Pathless
Self of Mystery

(see page 216)

Photo #44 ䷜
29

Liberated
Self of Mystery

(see page 218)

Photo #45 ䷐
17

Ecstatic Realization

Self of Mystery   (see page 221)

Photo #46 ䷚
25

Universal

Self of Mystery   (see page 222)

Photo #47 ䷗
4

All-encompassing
Self of Mystery

(see page 225)

Photo #48 ䷄

Identity

Self of Mystery

(see page 227)

7

Photo #49 ䷇

Nameless, Not Even

Self of Mind

(see page 241)

44

Photo #50 ䷗ 28

Buddha-nature

Self of Mind

(see page 242)

Photo #51 ䷗ 36

Abyss

Self of Mind

(see page 244)

Photo #52 ䷉ 22
Non-attaining, All-ness
Self of Mind   (see page 246)

Photo #53 ䷏ 50
Tao
Self of Mind   (see page 248)

Photo #54   ☰̶̶   Absolute
            32   Self of Mind   (see page 250)

Photo #55   ☰̶̶   Undivided
            63   Self of Mind   (see page 253)

Photo #56 ䷢ Non-clinging, Non-attachment
37   Self of Mind   (see page 254)

Photo #57 ䷞ Uncreated
55   Self of Onliness   (see page 269)

Photo #58 ䷝
30

No-separation, Oneness
Self of Onliness
(see page 270)

Photo #59 ䷵
57

Timeless
Self Of Onliness
(see page 272)

Photo #60 ䷁
48

Unfathomable
Self of Onliness

(see page 274)

Photo #61 ䷂
49

Unspeakable
Self of Onliness

(see page 277)

Photo #62 ䷂
13

Ultimate
Self of Onliness

(see page 278)

Photo #63 ䷒
18

All-present, No-ness
Self of Onliness

(see page 280)

Photo #64 ䷭ 46

Supreme
Self of Onliness   (see page 282)